MW00424439

"Nothing is more critical th          work of Jesus Christ. If w          everything else—the nature          ...p....es, and the church. This insightful volume from Dr. Nichols traces the doctrine of Christ in the earliest centuries of church history—showing that the truth about Christ's person and work goes back to Christ himself. In a world where the biblical depiction of Christ is often distorted or denied, this book serves as a tremendous defense of orthodox Christian belief. But its value is more than just apologetic. Its Christ-centered focus makes *For Us and for Our Salvation* a recommended read for anyone who wants a clear picture of the Savior."

> —JOHN A. MACARTHUR, Pastor-Teacher, Grace Community
> Church, Sun Valley, California

"With clarity and brevity, Stephen J. Nichols presents the intriguing development of the doctrine of Christ over the early centuries of the church. His account of the key councils and theological proposals is written in a very simple and readable style, and the reader is made aware of how much was at stake 'for us and for our salvation' in these very crucial debates. His inclusion of selections from primary sources and his very helpful glossary of key terms assist in making this vitally important period more understandable. As an overview of the key issues and developments involved in formulating the church's Christology, Nichols has provided a wonderfully clear and accessible introductory work."

> —BRUCE A. WARE, Professor of Christian Theology,
> Senior Associate Dean, School of Theology Advanced
> M.Div. Program Director, The Southern Baptist
> Theological Seminary

"By interweaving original sources and explanatory chapters, Nichols has given us a genre of historical theology that is both informative and interesting."

> —MILLARD ERICKSON, Distinguished Professor of Theology,
> Western Seminary, Portland

"In *For Us and for Our Salvation*, Stephen Nichols has given us a wonderfully readable book about one of the most important eras of the Christian church. Nichols guides us through the earliest centuries of Christian history, deftly navigating the Christological controversies, debates, heresies, and orthodox formulations. We hear the voices of Ignatius, Irenaeus, Athanasius, and many others as they defend, often 'against the world,' an orthodox Christology and the Trinitarian foundation of our faith. Whether you know this history well, or whether this is your first foray into the Christological debates of the first centuries, you will not want to put this book down. This is, however, not simply a report of what happened 'back then'—it is a book uniquely relevant to our own day, surrounded as we are by popular magazines, books, television shows, and movies (not to mention Arians literally knocking at our doors), all attempting to give us the definitive or 'scholarly' answer to the age-old question, 'Who is Jesus?' How that question is answered is no mere historical or academic debate—it is a matter of defending the faith once for all delivered to the saints. I would encourage everyone—pastors, teachers, students, and laymen—to 'take and read.'"

—BRIAN VICKERS, Assistant Professor of New Testament
Interpretation, The Southern Baptist Theological Seminary

"This book is a great idea and a valuable contribution to the church. Stephen Nichols provides a wise selection of classic excerpts on the doctrine of Christ, and he places them in the context of a readable story with helpful explanations that ordinary Christians can follow. In the daze of *The Da Vinci Code* and other revivals of ancient errors, we need clear celebrations of Christian orthodoxy such as this."

—DAN TREIER, Associate Professor of Theology,
Wheaton College

FOR US AND
FOR OUR SALVATION

STEPHEN J.
NICHOLS

*The Doctrine of Christ
in the Early Church*

# FOR US AND
# FOR OUR SALVATION

CROSSWAY BOOKS
WHEATON, ILLINOIS

**Library of Congress Cataloging-in-Publication Data**
Nichols, Stephen J., 1970–
    For us and for our salvation : the doctrine of Christ in the early church / Stephen J. Nichols.
        p. cm.
    ISBN 978-1-58134-867-5 (tpb)
    1. Jesus Christ—History of doctrines—Early church, ca. 30–600. I. Title.
BT198.N56        2007
232.09'015—dc22                                              2007003660

| VP |    | 17 | 16 | 15 | 14 | 13 | 12 | 11 | 10 | 09 | 08 | 07 |
|----|----|----|----|----|----|----|----|----|----|----|----|----|
| 15 | 14 | 13 | 12 | 11 | 10 | 9  | 8  | 7  | 6  | 5  | 4  | 3  | 2 | 1 |

*For*
GEORGE NICHOLS
JAMES KUTNOW
MICHAEL ROGERS

*in appreciation for*
*preaching Christ and him crucified*

# Contents

# Acknowledgments

I am very grateful for a circle of friends who are quick to offer encouragement and support. With the risk of missing some, I'd like to personally thank these folks for contributing directly and indirectly to this book: Eric Brandt, Mark Deckard, Allan Fisher, Gordon Gregory, Ted Griffin, Darryl Hart, Keith and Beverly Haselhorst, Keith Krueger, Timothy Larsen, Sean Lucas, Ray Naugle, Sam Storms, Justin Taylor, Derek Thomas, Carl Trueman, and my mom, Diane Nichols. I am especially grateful to Lester Hicks, Dale Mort, and Dan Treier for their close reading of the manuscript and for saving me the embarrassment of my mistakes. Some of my graduate students graciously endured being subjected to the manuscript. Thank you for courageously telling me when I didn't make sense.

My family has graciously settled in to losing me to the past from time to time. I am truly grateful. Thank you, Heidi, Ben, and Ian. Finally, this book is dedicated to the three pastors that I've had in my lifetime: George Nichols, my father; Jim Kutnow, who now ministers in Milan in the shadow of Ambrose's cathedral; and Michael Rogers, our pastor in Lancaster. Thank you for preaching Christ and him crucified. I think Athanasius is grateful to you too.

# "Who Do People Say That I Am?":
## Christ's Crucial Question

Thanks to a best-selling novel and to a movie with the likes of Tom Hanks, people everywhere inside the church and out are talking about the Nicene Creed, the Chalcedonian Creed, gnosticism, the Christology of the early church, and early church figures such as Irenaeus, Athanasius, and Arius. This is a theologian's dream scenario, and in some cases a nightmare scenario as well. Imagine the shock of reading three whole paragraphs about the Nicene Creed in the pages of *USA Today*. Before the *Da Vinci Code* phenomenon, you would be hard-pressed to find three paragraphs on the Nicene Creed in a Christian book, let alone in America's most read newspaper.

The overwhelming wake of *The Da Vinci Code* has, like a tropical storm, caused a great deal of damage. Yet, some good has come out of it, not the least of which is that people are talking about the Nicene Creed. What's more, Christians are talking about it too. And some of them are looking at it for the first time. All of this is good, very good, for the church. The Nicene and Chalcedonian Creeds express the bedrock of our faith. They put forth the biblical teaching of who Christ is and what he has done for us. This book's title, *For Us and for Our Salvation*, comes right from the Nicene Creed. It is a way of saying that who Christ is has everything to do with the gospel, the church's true treasure. If we learn anything from *The Da Vinci Code* phenomenon, it must be the lesson of the importance of getting the person of Christ right. The early church labored hard and long over this question, and they did so in the face of intense challenge. The contemporary church needs to do no less.

In our contemporary struggle to present Christ as the Bible portrays him, we should not work in a vacuum. We owe it to ourselves to look to the past and to learn from the church's struggles. Perhaps in no area of theology is this more necessary or beneficial than in the doctrine of Christ in the early church. The first four or five centuries of the church's existence witnessed the launch of nearly every possible challenge. Further, one is hard-pressed to offer a better response to those challenges than that offered by the early church leaders. We may be able to devise fresh and contemporary ways to illustrate their teachings and expressions, or we may have to think of new ways to relate their teachings to the particular challenges that we face in our day, but there is practically no room for improvement on those teachings. What these early church leaders said and did is tried and true.

The early church fathers wrestled with the same problems presented by *The Da Vinci Code* phenomenon and its fanciful speculations about Jesus. They wrestled with the same problems presented by Islam and its adamant denial of the deity of Christ. And they wrestled with the same problems presented by the scholars working in the Jesus Seminar or in gnostic texts like the Gospel of Judas who quickly dismiss the four canonical Gospels as God's true revelation to humanity. In the days of the early church, the names of the opponents were different from those faced by us today, but the underlying issues bear a striking resemblance. When the church fathers responded with the orthodox view of Christ, they did the church of all ages a great service.

This book explores these controversies over Christ faced by the early church. This book also looks to tell the story of the people involved—Arius and Eutyches, Ignatius and Irenaeus, Athanasius and Leo. These may or may not be known to contemporary evangelicals, but they should be. The following chapters unfold this struggle in the early church chronologically. Chapter 1 starts with one foot in the pages of the New Testament and stretches to the first decade of the 300s. Chapter 3 tells the story of Athanasius and his arch-nemesis Arius, the two figures behind the Nicene Council in 325 and the Council of Constantinople in 381. Chapter 5 unfolds the events of the 400s, focusing on Leo I and the Chalcedonian Council in 451. In an unprecedented event, no fewer than 520 bishops met and actually agreed on a very nuanced and sophisticated theological statement that we know as the Chalcedonian Creed. The intervening chapters, 2, 4, and 6, all break from the narrative to provide primary source documents, allowing the major figures in this struggle to tell the story in their own words. A brief epilogue explores the variations on these themes that have occurred in the life of the church since Chalcedon in 451.

The early church was right in spending so much time and effort on the doctrine of Christ. They were right to contend that Christ is the God-man, very God of very God and at the same time truly human with flesh and blood. They were right to contend that Christ is two natures conjoined in one person without division, separation, confusion, or mixture, to use the language of the Chalcedonian Creed. They were also right to contend that the gospel collapses without this belief. In the words of Athanasius and the Nicene Creed, Christ is the God-man *"for us and for our salvation."*

# In the Beginning Was the Word: Christ in the Early Centuries

*For in [Christ] the whole fullness of deity dwells bodily.*
COLOSSIANS 2:9

*For many deceivers have gone out into the world, those who do not confess the coming of Jesus Christ in the flesh. Such a one is the deceiver and the antichrist.*
2 JOHN 7

*In what way did he come but this, "The Word was made flesh and dwelt among us."*
AUGUSTINE, *ON CHRISTIAN DOCTRINE*

Even before we get out of the pages of the New Testament, Christ comes under fire. During his earthly life and public ministry, the crowds, the religious leaders, even at times his own chosen disciples got him wrong. His life of working miracles and his teaching of who he was and what he came to do were in plain view for everyone to see and hear. Despite this, he was misinterpreted, denied, and rejected. In the face of his healing, he was called the son of Satan (Matt. 12:22-32). In the face of his teaching, he was called the mere son of a carpenter (John 6:41-51). In the face of his death on the cross, he was mocked as the king of the Jews (John 19:19-22). And in the face of his resurrection, he was mistaken as a gardener (John 20:15). Fifty days after his death and after he had ascended back to heaven, Peter had to tell the crowd that Jesus, the very one whom they had seen and who had walked among them, was indeed *the* Christ, *the* Messiah, and that he was indeed *the* Lord (Acts 2:36). Those great crowds missed it, and, at least for a time, so had his closest followers. They had gotten him altogether wrong.

After his ascension and in the first decades of the church, the situation grew worse. The apostles and the early church contended with those teaching falsely about Christ. According to John, these false teachings centered around two poles. The first concerned the denial of Christ as the Messiah (1 John 2:22). The second concerned the denial of the incarnation, the teaching that Jesus was fully human and had truly come in the flesh (1 John 4:2; 2 John 7). These two poles of thought dominated not only the first century but the immediate following centuries. This chapter explores these false teachings and the response to them in the early church.

## *CHRISTOS* AND COBBLERS

Mr. Christ. At least that's the answer from the child in the Sunday school class to the teacher's question concerning the one born in a stable in Bethlehem. In the child's scheme of things, Jesus was the first name, Christ was the last. And, as his parents had taught him, he added the Mr. out of respect. Of course, in the case of Jesus, Christ is not the last name, it's a title. However, many, even those who should have known better, missed this. To them he was Jesus of Nazareth, or Jesus, the son of Joseph, the ancient versions of last names.[1] Acknowledging Jesus as *the* Christ, however, requires a great deal. The Greek word *Christos* means "anointed one" and is the counterpart to the Hebrew term meaning "Messiah." Designating Jesus as the Christ requires that one see him as the long-awaited Messiah, the anointed one of God, who would be the redeemer and deliverer of the covenant people. That Jesus assumed the title *Christ* in both word and deed is undeniable. That those in his day and in the centuries following his birth denied him as the Christ is undeniable too.

The denial of Jesus as the Christ began among the leaders of the Jewish community. Jesus of Nazareth disappointed them as a candidate for the Messiah. He lacked charisma and *gravitas*, not to mention an army. The Israelite nation was faced with occupation by the Roman Empire, and Jesus failed to fulfill their dreams of a conquering Messiah. The Jewish leaders' rejection of his claim to be their Messiah may be clearly seen in the exchange with Pontius Pilate. When that official ordered an inscription on the cross that would signify Christ's crime as claiming to be "Jesus of Nazareth, the King of the Jews," the Jewish leaders demanded that it be changed to read that he claimed to be the king of the Jews. Jesus claimed it, but they certainly did not want him. Pilate refused to change it (John 19:19-22).

One group in particular that was influenced by Jewish teachings denying the deity of Christ was the Ebionites. We don't know much about this group. Epiphanius, the fourth-century bishop of Salamis and later Cyprus, claims that Ebion founded this group. This may be a creative fiction. Other church fathers offered their own explanation of the name. The term likely comes from the Hebrew word for "poor." They were the "poor" disciples. Later opponents of them would use the name sarcastically to refer to their less than stellar mental capabilities, calling them "poor" thinkers. We also speculate that this group probably arose in the first century, likely coming into prominence after the destruction of Jerusalem in A.D. 70. The Ebionites were scattered from Jerusalem and Israel and congregated initially in Kochaba but soon spread throughout the empire. Scholars further tend to see this group as an extension of the Judaizers, the faction that Paul contended with in his Epistle to the Galatians. They were in effect trying to be Jewish Christians, not quite ready to accept the teachings of Paul or the book of Hebrews or John. All of which is to say that they were falling short of what constitutes true Christianity. It appears that the Ebionites were unable to sustain themselves in walking this tightrope between Judaism and Christianity. By the middle of the 400s they had virtually become extinct, some migrating to Judaism, others affirming orthodox Christianity.[2]

## HERESY

The English word *heresy* is a transliteration of both the Greek and Latin word. The Wycliffe Bible may contain the first occurrence of the English word, merely transliterating it from the Latin Vulgate at Acts 24:14. It occurs several times in the New Testament, initially meaning "sect" or "school of thought." The Sadducees and Pharisees are termed a sect in Acts 5:17 and 15:5. The term is also used to speak of the Christians themselves in Acts 24:14 and 28:22. In the epistles the term is used to refer to groups that are causing division in the church, such as the ESV translation of the word as "factions" in 1 Corinthians 11:19. By the later epistles, especially 2 Peter, the term comes to mean divisive groups within the church that are promoting false teaching. In 2 Peter 2:1 the ESV translates the term as "heresies," which are destructive and are brought into the church by false teachers. This particular heresy in 2 Peter centers on Christ. In the early church, teachings that went against Scripture were considered heresy, usually at synods. Once Christianity became legalized in the Roman Empire, a charge of heresy not only meant excommunication from the church but could also bring legal ramifications. As the church formulated and finalized the creeds, especially the Nicene and Chalcedonian Creeds, there became rather fixed and firm boundaries between heresy and orthodoxy. Augustine once said, in a rather lengthy letter dealing with heresy, that heretics "prefer their own contentions to the testimonies of Holy writ" and that they consequently separate themselves from the true, universal church.

Most of what we know about the Ebionites comes from the writings of the church fathers against them. Irenaeus mounted the first sustained refutation of them. He, in fact, was the first to use the name "Ebionites" in print, around 190. Hippolytus and Origen would later contribute their own refutations. The Ebionites viewed Christ as a prophet, and some of them even accepted the virgin birth. But they all denied his preexistence and consequently denied his deity. Eusebius, the first church historian, writing in 325, put the Ebionite heresy succinctly: "The adherents of what is known as the Ebionite heresy assert that Christ was the son of Joseph and Mary, and regard him as no more than a man." While viewing Jesus as a mere man, the Ebionites nevertheless exalted Jesus as one who kept the law perfectly, and as a group they stressed the keeping of the law in order to attain salvation. Like the Judaizers of Paul's day, they insisted on circumcision. Their faulty view of Christ led to a faulty view of Christ's work on the cross. Their misunderstanding of the incarnation led to a misunderstanding of the atonement. They did not grasp the fact that Christ is the God-man who is for us. This fact makes all the difference for our salvation.[3]

Another and more sophisticated view that denied Christ's *Adoptians* deity circulated in the early church. This view, called adoptionism, held that God adopted the human Jesus as his son after he was born, either at Jesus' baptism or at his resurrection. When the one God descended on the human Jesus, Jesus became the son of God and became the Christ, filled with divine power. Eusebius refers to this as "Artemon's heresy." We, however, know nothing of Artemon beyond this brief reference. Later proponents of this teaching include Paul of Samasota (third century) and Theodotus (c. 190). Theodotus the Cobbler—to distinguish him from the other Theodotuses in church history—arrived in Rome around 190 and began spreading adoptionist teachings. The church excommunicated Theodotus, and his followers floundered. Paul of Samasota was able to gain a little more traction due to his being bishop at Antioch. Around 260 he was declared a heretic for his adoptionist view in a synod at Antioch. Eusebius gives us the report: "The other pastors of the churches from all directions, made haste to assemble at Antioch, as against a despoiler of the flock of Christ." It was in the course of dealing with his teaching in three different synods that the term *homoousios* came into play (much more on this term, which means that Christ is of the same essence as the Father, in Chapter 3).[4]

The views of these adoptionists are a subset of a larger group of heresies under the umbrella term of *monarchianism,* which refers to "one" ruler or one God. The monarchians put all the emphasis on the oneness of God. They were unable to see the other side, the three persons of the Godhead. They believed that the Bible teaches about Christ and even about the Holy Spirit. They understood these teachings, however, to refer to modes of being of the one God; Christ and the Holy Spirit were manifestations of this one God. They would speak of *patripassionism,* which literally means that God the Father (the Latin word is *pater*) was the one who was suffering on the cross (*pathos* or *passion* means "suffering"). Jesus Christ and God the Father are not separate persons, they said. Rather, Jesus Christ is a mere manifestation of God. One teacher of this heresy was Praxeas, known to us only through the writings of his opponent, Tertullian. Some think "Praxeas" to be a nickname. We know that he was a figure who arrived at Rome some time around 200. Another advocate of patripassionism was Sabellius, who also taught this view in Rome in the first two decades of the 200s. Sabellius was excommunicated in 217, but the movement he founded, known as Sabellianism, appeared in various places in the ensuing centuries.[5]

The views of the Ebionites and adoptionists were only the first ripples of the heresies that would deny Christ's deity and would come to dominate the 300s. These views, however, seemed eclipsed by the damage done by controversies over Christ's humanity. Pilate, in addition to identifying Christ as the King of the Jews, also rather insightfully said of Christ, "Behold the man!" (John 19:5; *Ecce homo* in Latin). Many, however, were not ready or willing to see him as truly in the flesh. "It is his flesh," Tertullian would say, "that is the problem." Thus, in the first and second centuries Christ's humanity dominated the

*Philosophical effect on Theology (like Postmodernism today)*

discussion. (This makes sense given the philosophical climate of those first two centuries. Plato's ideas dominated the intellectual world of both scholars and the populace alike.) A fundamental doctrine of Platonic philosophy conflicts with the doctrine of the incarnation. For Plato, matter is bad, while the ideal is good. The body is bad, while the soul is good and pure. In Greek a catchy little jingle catches this well: *Soma toma*. Translated, it means: "Body, tomb." If they'd had bumper stickers, this saying would have been on the chariots of the Platonist philosophers. For a Platonist, being in the flesh was not worth celebrating. Instead Platonists viewed the flesh as an inconvenient impediment that someday, when the body lies in the grave, will be overcome. Jesus coming in the flesh, the incarnation, embarrasses those who like their Platonism. His incarnation becomes quite the stumbling block.[6]

One of Plato's more popular dialogues causes even more problems for the doctrine of the incarnation. In *Timeaus*, Plato takes a stab at explaining the big questions of life: Where did everything come from? Where did I come from? He answers by first running through mythological explanations such as the phoenix myth or the Atlantis myth, with most scholars understanding the Atlantis myth as Plato's creative invention. Then Plato posits what appears to be his own explanation for the world and all things in it. Plato's cosmology, or understanding of the world, starts with the abstract form, or what he prefers to call The Ideal. This Ideal, or God—but Plato would prefer to keep this figure impersonal and not personal—then created a buffer god, whom Plato calls the *Demiurge*, which means a creator god. The *Demiurge* in turn created all things. But even here there's a flow chart. Plato thought males to be superior to females, females to be superior to animals, animals to be superior to flora and fauna, flora and fauna to be superior to stones and dirt. Matter is at the bottom of the chain, idea and the immaterial at the top. The farther down the chain, the lesser the value, the lesser the meaning.[7]

**PLATO'S COSMOLOGY**

The Ideal

§

The Demiurge (creator god)

§

The World, Humanity, and Matter

-----------

Males

§

Females

§

Animals

§

Flora and Fauna

§

Rocks and Dirt

The biblical cosmology differs from Plato's on another count. For Plato, this world of matter matters very little. As the physical body cages the human soul, the physical world cages the *forms*. Things represent instantiations of the forms, which represent The Form or The Ideal. Now this needs some unpacking. Again, at the top of the chain is The Ideal, the ultimate reality. The Ideal then is represented in various ideas or forms, like the forms of justice, beauty, or truth, or even the forms of personhood or of different animals. These forms then are represented in the world in individual, material things, like the things of laws, art, and science, or like the things of different human beings or dogs or cats.[8] —Created by the Demiurge

You might still be lost, so consider dogs as an example. There are many, many different dogs. Some are little, while some are large, like a Chihuahua versus a mastiff. Some are trained for certain functions, like herding animals or protection, while others seem destined to spend their days chasing their tails. Yet, all of these different creatures are all called *dog*. Plato explains this by arguing that all of these creatures are physical manifestations of the form of dog—they are all individual, material occurrences of the immaterial form or idea (although I don't think he called it *dogginess*). When dogs cease to exist materially, the essence of the dog returns to the world of the forms. So it is with human beings. Of different colors, sizes, and shapes, all humans are material occurrences of the form of humanity. When we cease to exist in our physical lives, our souls reunite with the world of the forms.

Among the many implications of this understanding of the world stands the idea that this world matters little. This world functions as a vehicle back to the world of the forms. It is to be escaped from; it is to be overcome. Nothing of value comes from material things. *Soma toma*—the body is a tomb. The Bible poses a different worldview, a worldview that sees this world as having meaning, that sees the physical as a gift from God. When God surveyed the world he made, he pronounced it good, *very* good, in fact. The biblical creation account finds God grabbing a handful of dust and breathing into it, creating a being of matter and spirit with whom he desired to fellowship. And, due to humanity's sin, Jesus, the divine son, humbled himself, took on flesh, and became human. Plato has no room for the incarnation. It belittles The Ideal to even consider having it take on flesh.

Now we see why the doctrine of the incarnation faced challenges in the first few centuries. The idea that God would take on flesh proved unpalatable to Platonic tastes. To a Platonist, the incarnation smacked of unsophisticated, elementary thinking. In order to keep Platonism on the one hand and to keep some semblance of Christianity on the other required an adjustment. Jesus, it was held, did not really take on flesh; he only *appeared* to take on flesh. The Greek word for "appear" is *dokeo*, which gives this false teaching its name of *docetism*. Docetism is the teaching that Jesus only appeared in the flesh and was not truly human. Unlike some of the other heresies looked at in later chapters, this heresy was not necessarily associated with a single individual. Instead this heresy popped up in various forms, in various groups, throughout the early church's life. Even today it manages to find mild expression in the tendency to view Jesus as sort of floating six inches off the ground as he walked upon the earth. Instead of any docetic understanding of Christ, the Bible presents Christ as hungry, thirsty, and tired. As the ultimate testimony to his full humanity, the Bible presents him as dying on a cross.

In those first few centuries, however, there was nothing mild about the form that docetism took. John informs us in his epistles that its adherents denied that Jesus had come in the flesh, that his humanity amounted to nothing more than a mask, a costume. He appeared to eat, he appeared to drink, and he appeared to go through the cycles of human development. He appeared to have bled, and he only appeared to have died in the flesh. Against this view, the author of Hebrews declares that Jesus had to be made like us, fully human in the flesh, in order for his death to have any significance. He is a faithful high priest because he is one of us (Heb. 2:17). This teaching echoes Paul's insistence that Christ was like us in every respect, except of course that he knew no sin (2 Cor. 5:21). Pilate put it this way: "Behold the man!" (John 19:5; *Ecce homo* in Latin). But when the docetists looked, they didn't see a human being of flesh and blood.

## DOCETISM

Valentinus (c. 136–c. 165) became one of the leaders of the docetists. Most of what we know about Valentinus comes to us from his theological opponent Irenaeus, who wrote no less than a five-volume work against Valentinus and his followers, who were called Valentinians. We have come to call Irenaeus's work *Against Heresies* (*Adversus Haereses*). From it we can reconstruct Valentinus's teachings along the following lines. In the beginning there was the eternal Father, who dwelled alone in silence and with his thoughts—a dream world for a Platonist. This Father is incomprehensible, entirely transcendent. His silence eventually becomes realized in mind and thought, forming the first of thirty pairs of "aeons," which are set off like a chain reaction. Eventually *Sophia* is produced, whose offspring is the *Demiurge* (Plato's word) who creates the material world. Valentinus took this *Demiurge* to be the God of the Old Testament. The "aeon" of Christ united with the human form Jesus to show humanity the way of salvation. While all this may sound like bad science fiction, it resonated enough with the Platonism of the day to get a following. Readers of *The Da Vinci Code* will immediately recognize the term *Sophia*. Thanks to Valentinus and others, this *Sophia* teaching found a home in gnosticism.[9]

The Valentinians considered themselves to be the enlightened ones who possessed this secret knowledge and entered the fullness, which they termed "pleroma" after the Greek word. They viewed other Christians, who lacked such enlightenment, as "psychic," while they understood non-Christians to be merely material and doomed to eternal perdition. There were three classes of people—the spiritual, the ensouled (psychic), and the earthly. This, it is held, is taught in the Bible, with Cain, Abel, and Seth being the originators of these three classes.[10]

All the elements of heresy may be found in Valentinus and the Valentinians. First, we see how heresy retools biblical teaching, conforming it to other ways of thinking rather than vice versa. In this case Plato's doctrines of matter and idea, as well as his cosmology, form the starting point for understanding what, if any, contribution biblical teaching makes to an understanding of the world. Second, we see how once a system has a faulty starting point, it sets off a chain reaction of false teachings. Heresy on one point, in other words, tends to beget heresy on others, which beget heresy on others still. Thirdly, we see how heresies set up sects or groups of people who have a privileged status, having been enlightened, and are above others. This overinflated sense of their own selves is what tended to make the heretics so divisive in the early church.

Topping the list of docetists in the early centuries is Marcion (d. 160). Marcion, the son of a bishop, shifted so radically from Christianity that he eventually set up a rival church. Platonism so influenced his thinking that he nearly dismissed the whole Old Testament because it dealt so much with earthly affairs. The Gospels also came under his knife. Any elements that were too reflective of the Old Testament were gone, as were those elements that stressed the material and physical. Marcion cut out the birth narratives of Jesus altogether. His Jesus floats down out of the sky at the wedding at Capernaum. (No wonder they ran out of wine.) Marcion managed to gather quite a following, probably due to his emphasis on what he called the gospel of love versus the gospel of law. For him, grace ruled. He was excommunicated from the church in Rome in 144. Possessing great wealth, he managed to establish quite a network of followers and churches, whose influence was sadly felt throughout the next centuries.

One thing Marcion's heresy prompted was the church's recognition of the canon of the Old Testament, since Marcion was denying practically all of it. The other thing it set off was a full-blown defense of the humanity of Christ, since Marcion was denying that too. Tertullian led the charge against him, writing *Against Marcion* in 207–208. This work consisted of five books that laid out Marcion's teachings before dismantling them. Tertullian explains hypothetically what's at stake in Marcion's denial of Christ's humanity: "The sufferings of Christ will be found not to warrant faith in him. For he suffered nothing who did not truly suffer; and a phantom could not truly suffer. God's entire work therefore is subverted. Christ's death, wherein lies the whole weight and fruit of the Christian name, is denied." Tertullian continues to tease out the implication of

Marcion, noting that if Jesus was not in the flesh, he did not live, die, or rise again in the flesh, "and so our faith is in vain." Tertullian then counters Marcion's teaching by referring to Paul: "The Apostle asserts [Christ's humanity] so expressly and undoubtedly real, making it the very foundation of the gospel, of our salvation, and of his own preaching." Christ truly came in the flesh.[11]

## THE I'S HAVE IT

In addition to Tertullian, two others emerge in these battles for Christ in the first centuries: Ignatius and Irenaeus. Ignatius (b. ?–d. 110s) was bishop of Antioch, the city where the followers of Christ were first called Christians. Ignatius, too, used that term quite often. He also preferred Jesus the Christ as the way to speak of Christ. While we do not see in his writings the thorough and specific language of a two-nature Christology that would eventually come out of Chalcedon (451), we see him stressing the deity of Christ and the humanity of Christ in his seven epistles.[12]

In his *Epistle to the Trallians* (to the church at Tralles in Asia), he writes of Christ as one "who was really born, who both ate and drank; who really was persecuted under Pontius Pilate, who really was crucified and died." In his letter to the church at Smyrna, he speaks of Christ as being "truly" born, persecuted, and crucified. Ignatius uses "really" and "truly" to contradict the term "apparently" as used by the docetists when speaking of Christ's humanity. It mattered no less to Ignatius that Christ was God. He speaks of Jesus Christ as God in his letter to the churches in Smyrna and in Ephesus. His letters, all of which were penned around 110, reveal the firm belief of the early church in the deity and humanity of Christ. To be sure, the church would articulate these beliefs with more clarity and precision in the ensuing centuries. Nevertheless, the argument that the belief in the humanity and deity of Christ did not come about until the 300s, as some scholars and *The Da Vinci Code* claim, is patently false.[13]

## CHAPTER ONE SCORECARD

| The Good | The Bad |
|---|---|
| Ignatius (d. 107) | the Ebionites (c. 70–400s) |
| Irenaeus (130–202) | Marcion (d. 160) |
| Tertullian (c. 200s) | Valentinus (136–165) |
| Hippolytus (170–236) | Theodotus the Cobbler (c. 190) |
| | Paul of Samasota (c. 200s) |
| | Sabellius (c. 200) |

Ignatius should be much better known than he is among contemporary Christians. His letters not only offer these teachings of Christ we've been emphasizing, they also give us a sense of the early church's view of Scripture. When Ignatius wants to make a point, he quotes Paul. When he really wants to make a point, he quotes a whole string of Paul. We also see in Ignatius's letters the structure of offices in the early church. Ignatius lays out instructions for bishops, elders, and deacons, in that order. Finally, we should remember Ignatius for the sacrifice he made to the church. He wrote to these churches because he visited them firsthand—on his way to Rome as a prisoner. When he arrived in Rome, he was martyred by the emperor Trajan. Ignatius knew how important the doctrine of Christ was to the church, and he knew the gravity of the docetist threat. Before he died, he wanted to put these thoughts on paper.

Equally alarmed by the threat to the doctrine of Christ, Irenaeus (c. 115–c. 202) also took to writing in defense of the faith. He sat under the teaching of Polycarp, the bishop of Smyrna who was martyred in 156. Irenaeus eventually made it to Lyons, France, where he became bishop. He devoted his life to peacekeeping missions within the church. For him, keeping the peace meant not only striving for unity but also weeding out heresy. The gnostic Valentinus and his followers, the Valentinians, as mentioned earlier, found out just how capable and dedicated Irenaeus could be in defending Christian beliefs. Irenaeus's *Against Heresies* aimed at not only deconstructing these false teachings but also laying out for the church the proper biblical understanding of the doctrines of God, humanity, creation, incarnation, and resurrection.[14]

He stressed the oneness and unity of God, while at the same time offering an early teaching of the Trinity. Tertullian would coin that term, and the Cappadocian Fathers (see Chapter 5) along with Augustine would later give it full-blown development. Yet the basic understanding of the doctrine is found in Irenaeus's work. Irenaeus understood Christ to be the fully divine Son of God who became the fully human son of Mary at the incarnation. He stood against gnosticism's diminished view of humanity. For Irenaeus, the God-man Christ lived and died, and the God-man Christ rose again. Consequently, Christ vindicates life in the flesh.

In Book One of *Against Heresies*, Irenaeus declares that the apostles proclaimed "the one Jesus Christ, the Son of God, who was enfleshed [incarnated] for our Salvation." He then refers to Jesus Christ as "our Lord and God, Savior and King." Irenaeus takes it a step further, noting that if anyone were "to preach to [the apostles] the inventions of the heretics . . . they would at once stop their ears and flee as far off as possible, not enduring even to listening to the blasphemous address." Irenaeus is saying in the strongest language possible that the teachings of the docetists and the gnostics are diametrically opposed to the teachings of the Bible.[15]

Irenaeus's life, like Ignatius's, felt the cruel hand of Roman persecution. While an elder at Lyons, he was sent to Rome by the bishop of Lyons to convey a message. During his absence an intense persecution occurred at Lyons and the neighboring city of Vienne. When Irenaeus returned, he found the majority of the church, including the bishop, martyred, while others had fled the city. Irenaeus was appointed bishop and set about rebuilding the church there. Through his writings, his influence extended far beyond that city. And through his discipleship of Hippolytus, his influence extended beyond his lifetime.

An early translator of Hippolytus's work put it this way: "Hippolytus was a disciple of St. Irenaeus, St. Irenaeus of St. Polycarp, St. Polycarp of St. John." Hippolytus (c. 170–236) was a presbyter at Rome. He attacked the teaching of Sabellius, referred to earlier. He also disagreed with Rome's bishop, Calixtus I. Hippolytus, by all accounts, should have been the bishop, but Calixtus I was too entrenched in the church and too well connected. It mattered little, actually, for in a few years both Hippolytus and Calixtus I would be exiled by the emperor to the island of Sardinia. Since it wasn't clear to the emperor who was really in charge, he simply exiled them both. Legend has it that the two reconciled during the exile. Hippolytus died in Sardinia in 236.[16]

While exceptionally prolific in his own day, Hippolytus fell from attention shortly after his death all the way until 1551, when a statue was discovered during the excavation of one of Rome's ancient churches. The marble statue is of Hippolytus seated upon a chair. On one side of the base there is a list of all of his writings, writings that had been lost to history. It would be another three centuries until, in the 1840s, some of his manuscripts were discovered in the monastery at Mount Athos in Greece. Among these writings the most significant is the rather ambitiously titled *The Refutation of All Heresies*. And indeed it is. He starts with the Greek philosophers and then runs through all of the heresies, including the docetists and Ebionites, Marcion and Theodotus the Cobbler. He then concludes with a discussion of "The Doctrine of Truth." In it Hippolytus declares that Christ is both truly human—"He even underwent toil, and was willing to endure hunger, and did not refuse to feel thirst, and sunk into the quietude of slumber"—and truly God—"Christ is God above all." And then Hippolytus adds that the God-man has "arranged to wash away the sin of human beings."[17]

## CONCLUSION

As mentioned in the beginning of this chapter, even before we get out of the pages of the New Testament we see the two poles of heresies related to the person of Christ—denial of his deity and denial of his humanity. In the first three centuries of the church, controversy over Christ's humanity dominated the discussion. The docetists, imbibing way too much Platonism for their own good, simply could not allow for a human, fleshly Christ. Their view of God wouldn't allow it. Perhaps that shouldn't surprise us all that much. The inimitable Martin Luther was amazed by all paradoxes. But the paradox that amazed him the most was that the God of the universe would deign to take on flesh and be born in a stable. It further amazed the Reformer that the God-man Christ would suffer and die on the cross. He who made all things and rules the universe was bound and put to death. Luther marveled at it all. Others, like the docetists and the Sabellians, stumbled over it. They were met, however, with those committed to the teaching of the apostles and to the true church. *JW's today*

We shouldn't forget that while Ignatius, Irenaeus, Tertullian, Hippolytus, and others were laboring for the truth, they were doing so in a hostile environment. Christianity was illegal in the first few centuries, leaving Christians and the church's leaders open to persecution. The church faced challenges both from without by the empire and from within by the heretics. In 312 the tide would change as Constantine would reverse the attack on the church. No longer faced with the enemy from without, the church would still have to contend with the enemy within. And as we'll see in the next chapters, the doctrine of Christ would be at the center of the controversies swirling about.

## CHAPTER TWO

# In Their Own Words:
## Select Documents from the
## Early Centuries

The readings in this chapter supplement the narrative of Chapter 1. Many of the actual writings of the heretics have been lost to history, their views being preserved mainly in the polemical works of the early church fathers. A number of the apocryphal or pseudepigraphal (writings falsely attributed to the apostles or biblical authors) have survived. These include the recently popular *Gospel of Thomas*, from which a selection is given below. Also included here is a selection from *The Gospel of Truth*. This chapter, however, primarily showcases the work of Ignatius, Irenaeus, Tertullian, and Hippolytus, the major contenders for the orthodox view of Christ in the second through the fourth centuries. The early bishops wrote letters and book-length treatments on the issues facing the church, namely the heresies. These writings display a concern for the church to pattern itself after biblical teaching and to avoid the snares of heresies. The selections all evidence a firsthand knowledge of the intricacies of the heresies, as well as a strong commitment to the biblical portrait of Christ. For these church fathers, proclaiming the biblical view of Christ and refuting heretical views of Christ topped the agenda.

Introductions to these texts provide some information on the context of these selections. Notes are also included to help contemporary readers get a better handle on tricky points in these ancient texts. These samples are but the tip of the iceberg of the rich literary legacy of the early church. The early fathers went to great lengths to see that the church thought and believed properly about the person of Christ, so that it in turn accurately and persuasively proclaimed the gospel of Christ.

## GNOSTIC TEXTS

In 1949 at Nag Hammadi in Upper Egypt, archaeologists uncovered a library of thirteen leather-bound books containing more than fifty gnostic texts, among them the famed *Gospel of Thomas*. These texts represent the heresies of the first few centuries, evidencing a Platonist worldview and philosophy. In this selection from *The Gospel of Thomas* "Jesus" refers to the secret keys of knowledge that the Pharisees have hidden. Jesus will reveal these keys to his followers when they can get beyond their fleshly existence, evidenced in disrobing "without being ashamed." The last selection reveals the gnostic view that the physical universe is but a corpse, just as the body is the corpse of the soul.

The next text, *The Gospel of Truth*, is thought by some scholars to be written by Valentinus, discussed in Chapter 1. If not by him, it certainly comes from within his group of followers, the Valentinians. The brief selections here reveal their understanding of Christ and salvation, both of which have been hijacked by the Platonic ideal of pure rationality.

*The Gospel of Thomas; date: late second century; source: "The Gospel of Thomas (II, 2)," The Nag Hammadi Library in English, James M. Robinson, ed. (San Francisco: Harper & Row, 1988), 130-132.*

(37) His disciples said, "When will you become revealed to us and when shall we see you?" Jesus said, "When you disrobe without being ashamed and take up your garments and place them under your feet like little children and tread on them,

then [you will see] the son of the living one, and you will not be afraid. . . ."

(39) Jesus said, "The Pharisees and the scribes have taken the keys of knowledge [*gnosis*] and hidden them. They themselves have not entered, nor have they allowed those to enter who wish to. You, however, be as wise as serpents and as innocent as doves."

(56) Jesus said, "Whoever has come to understand the world has found (only) a corpse, and whoever has found a corpse is superior to the world."[1]

*The Gospel of Truth; date: c. 170; source: After the New Testament: A Reader in Early Christianity, Bart D. Ehrman, ed. (Oxford: Oxford University Press, 1999), 163-164.*

Truth appeared; all its emanations knew it. They greeted the Father in truth with a perfect power that joins them with the Father. For, as for everyone who loves the truth—because the truth is the mouth of the Father; his tongue is the Holy Spirit—he who is joined to the truth is joined to the Father's mouth by his tongue, whenever he is to receive the Holy Spirit, since this is the manifestation of the Father and his revelation to his aeons. . . .[2]

When [the Son] had appeared instructing them about the Father, the incomprehensible one, when he had breathed into them what is in the thought, doing his will, when many had received the light, they turned to him. For the material ones were strangers and did not see his likeness and had not known him. For he came by means of fleshly form, while nothing blocked his course[,] for incorruptibility is irresistible, since he, again, spoke new things, still speaking about what is in the heart of the Father, having brought forth the flawless word.[3]

When light had spoken through his mouth, as well as his voice which gave birth to life, he gave them thought and understanding and mercy and salvation and the powerful spirit from the infiniteness and the sweetness of the Father.

## EARLY CHURCH FATHERS
## IGNATIUS (B. ?-D. 110S)

Ignatius's *Epistles* give much insight into life in the early church. The selections here revolve around heresies concerning Christ and Ignatius's response to those heresies. The refutations of the later church fathers are much more complex, revealing that the heresies themselves underwent quite an evolution. The basic heresy Ignatius contended with was an early form of docetism, which denied that Jesus had come in the flesh. Ignatius refutes it as being unbiblical. He also shows how denial of Jesus' incarnation undermines his work on the cross in providing salvation.

*Ignatius, The Epistle to the Trallians, Chapters 9-10; date: c. 110; source: The Ante-Nicene Fathers, Vol. I: The Apostolic Fathers with Justin Martyr and Irenaeus, A. Cleveland Coxe, ed. (Grand Rapids, MI: Eerdmans, 1957), 69-71.*

Chapter 9: Stop your ears, therefore, when any one speaks to you at variance with Jesus Christ, who was descended from David, and was also of Mary; who was truly born, and did eat and drink. He was truly persecuted under Pontius Pilate; He was truly crucified, and died, in the sight of beings in heaven, and on earth, and under the earth. He was also truly raised from the dead, His Father quickening Him, even as after the same manner His Father will so raise up us who believe in Him by Christ Jesus, apart from whom we do not possess the true life.

Stop your ears, therefore, when any one speaks to you at variance with Jesus Christ, the Son of God, who was descended from David, and was also of Mary; who was truly begotten of God and of the Virgin, but not after the same manner. For indeed God and man are not the same. He truly assumed a body; for "the Word was made flesh," and lived upon earth without sin. For says He, "Which of you convicts me of sin?" He did in reality both eat and drink. He was crucified and died under Pontius Pilate. He really, and not merely in appearance,

Answer to Docetism

was crucified, and died, in the sight of beings in heaven, and on earth, and under the earth. By those in heaven I mean such as are possessed of incorporeal natures; by those on earth, the Jews and Romans, and such persons as were present at that time when the Lord was crucified; and by those under the earth, the multitude that arose along with the Lord. For says the Scripture, "Many bodies of the saints that slept arose," their graves being opened. He descended, indeed, into Hades alone, but He arose accompanied by a multitude; and rent asunder that means of separation which had existed from the beginning of the world, and cast down its partition-wall. He also rose again in three days, the Father raising Him up; and after spending forty days with the apostles, He was received up to the Father, and "sat down at His right hand, expecting till His enemies are placed under His feet." On the day of the preparation, then, at the third hour, He received the sentence from Pilate, the Father permitting that to happen; at the sixth hour He was crucified; at the ninth hour He gave up the ghost; and before sunset He was buried. During the Sabbath He continued under the earth in the tomb in which Joseph of Arimathaea had laid Him. At the dawning of the Lord's Day He arose from the dead, according to what was spoken by Himself, "As Jonah was three days and three nights in the whale's belly, so shall the Son of man also be three days and three nights in the heart of the earth." The day of the preparation, then, comprises the passion; the Sabbath embraces the burial; the Lord's Day contains the resurrection.

Chapter 10: But if, as some that are without God, that is, the unbelieving, say, that He only seemed to suffer (they themselves only seeming to exist), then why am I in bonds? Why do I long to be exposed to the wild beasts? Do I therefore die in vain? Am I not then guilty of falsehood against the cross of the Lord?[4]

But if, as some that are without God, that is, the unbelieving, say, He became man in appearance, that He did not in reality take unto Him a body, that He died in appearance, and did not in very deed suffer, then for what reason am I now in bonds, and long to be exposed to the wild beasts? In such a case, I die in vain, and am guilty of falsehood against the cross of the Lord. Then also does the prophet in vain declare, "They shall look on Him whom they have pierced, and mourn over themselves as over one beloved." These men, therefore, are not less unbelievers than were those that crucified Him. But as for me, I do not place my hopes in one who died for me in appearance, but in reality. For that which is false is quite abhorrent to the truth. Mary then did truly conceive a body which had God inhabiting it. And God the Word was truly born of the Virgin, having clothed Himself with a body of like passions with our own. He who forms all men in the womb, was Himself really in the womb, and made for Himself a body of the seed of the Virgin, but without any intercourse of man. He was carried in the womb, even as we are, for the usual period of time; and was really born, as we also are; and was in reality nourished with milk, and partook of common meat and drink, even as we do. And when He had lived among men for thirty years, He was baptized by John, really and not in appearance; and when He had preached the Gospel three years, and done signs and wonders, He who was Himself the Judge was judged by the Jews, falsely so called, and by Pilate the governor; was scourged, was smitten on the cheek, was spit upon; He wore a crown of thorns and a purple robe; He was condemned: He was crucified in reality, and not in appearance, not in imagination, not in deceit. He really died, and was buried, and rose from the dead, even as He prayed in a certain place, saying, "But do Thou, O Lord, raise me up again, and I shall recompense them." And the Father, who always hears Him, answered and said, "Arise, O God, and judge the earth; for Thou shall receive all the heathen for Thine inheritance." The Father, therefore, who raised Him up, will also raise us up through Him, apart from whom no one will attain to true life. For says He, "I am the life; he that believes in me, even though he die, shall live: and every one that lives and believes in me, even though he die, shall live for ever." Do ye therefore flee from these ungodly heresies; for they are the inventions of the devil, that serpent who was the author of evil, and who by means of the woman deceived Adam, the father of our race.

*Ignatius, The Epistle to the Smyrneans, Chapters 2-4; date: c. 110; source: The Ante-Nicene Fathers, Vol. I, 87-88.*

Chapter 2: Now, He suffered all these things for our sakes, that we might be saved.[5] And <u>He suffered truly, even as also He truly raised up Himself, not, as certain unbelievers maintain, that He only seemed to suffer, as they themselves only seem to be Christians</u>. And as they believe, so shall it happen unto them, when they shall be divested of their bodies, and be mere evil spirits.

Now, He suffered all these things for us; and He suffered them really, and not in appearance only, even as also He truly rose again. But not, as some of the unbelievers, who are ashamed of the formation of man, and the cross, and death itself, affirm, that in appearance only, and not in truth, He took a body of the Virgin, and suffered only in appearance, forgetting, as they do, Him who said, "The Word was made flesh"; and again, "Destroy this temple, and in three days I will raise it up"; and once more, "If I be lifted up from the earth, I will draw all men unto Me." The Word therefore did dwell in flesh, for "Wisdom built herself a house." The Word raised up again His own temple on the third day, when it had been destroyed by the Jews fighting against Christ. The Word, when His flesh was lifted up, after the manner of the brazen serpent in the wilderness, drew all men to Himself for their eternal salvation.

Chapter 3: For I know that after His resurrection also He was still possessed of flesh, and I believe that He is so now. When, for instance, He came to those who were with Peter, He said to them, "Lay hold, handle Me, and see that I am not an incorporeal spirit." And immediately they touched Him, and believed, being convinced both by His flesh and spirit. For this cause also they despised death, and were found its conquerors. And after his resurrection He did eat and drink with them, as being possessed of flesh, although spiritually He was united to the Father.

And I know that He was possessed of a body not only in His being born and crucified, but I also know that He was so after His resurrection, and believe that He is so now. When, for instance, He came to those who were with Peter, He said to them, "Lay hold, handle Me, and see that I am not an incorporeal spirit." "For a spirit hath not flesh and bones, as ye see Me have." And He says to Thomas, "Reach hither thy finger into the print of the nails, and reach hither thy hand, and thrust it into My side"; and immediately they believed that He was Christ. Wherefore Thomas also says to Him, "My Lord, and my God." And on this account also did they despise death, for it were too little to say, indignities and stripes. Nor was this all; but also after He had shown Himself to them, that He had risen indeed, and not in appearance only, He both ate and drank with them during forty entire days. And thus was He, with the flesh, received up in their sight unto Him that sent Him, being with that same flesh to come again, accompanied by glory and power. For, say the holy oracles, "This same Jesus, who is taken up from you into heaven, shall so come, in like manner as ye have seen Him go unto heaven." But if they say that He will come at the end of the world without a body, how shall those "see Him that pierced Him," and when they recognize Him, "mourn for themselves?" For incorporeal beings have neither form nor figure, nor the aspect of an animal possessed of shape, because their nature is in itself simple.

Chapter 4: I give you these instructions, beloved, assured that ye also hold the same opinions [as I do]. But I guard you beforehand from those beasts in the shape of men, whom you must not only not receive, but, if it be possible, not even meet with; only you must pray to God for them, if by any means they may be brought to repentance, which, however, will be very *Effectual* difficult. Yet <u>Jesus Christ, who is our true life, has the power of</u> *Grace* <u>effecting this</u>. But if these things were done by our Lord only in appearance, then am I also only in appearance bound. And why have I also surrendered myself to death, to fire, to the sword, to the wild beasts? But, he who is near to the sword is near to God; he that is among the wild beasts is in company with God; provided only he be so in the name of Jesus Christ. I undergo all these things that I may suffer together with Him, He who became a perfect man inwardly strengthening me.

I give you these instructions, beloved, assured that ye also hold the same opinions. But I guard you beforehand from these beasts in the shape of men, from whom you must not only turn away, but even flee from them. Only you must pray for them, if by any means they may be brought to repentance. For if the Lord were in the body in appearance only, and were crucified in appearance only, then am I also bound in appearance only. And why have I also surrendered myself to death, to fire, to the sword, to the wild beasts? But, I endure all things for Christ, not in appearance only, but in reality, that I may suffer together with Him, while <u>He Himself inwardly strengthens me; for of myself I have no such ability.</u>

## IRENAEUS (C. 130-C. 200)

We have a detailed account of Valentinus, as well as many other heresies of a gnostic kind, in the writings of Irenaeus. In addition to referencing the heretics themselves, Irenaeus also references the various pseudepigraphal texts of the gnostics, the so-called "lost gospels" that have captured so much attention today. <u>They were well-known in the early church, and they were</u> <u>also well-known to be patently false</u> (Irenaeus stresses that there are only four Gospels, four "Pillars," as he calls them. The selections here come from Books I and III of *Against the Heresies*.) He helps us see the connections between Plato's thought and the heretics. He also helps us see what's at stake in the church's understanding of Christ.

*Irenaeus, Against the Heresies (Adversus Haereses), Books I and III; date: c. 180; source: The Ante-Nicene Fathers, Vol. I, 322, 329-330, 428-429.*

Book I, Chapter 5, Section 1 (322):

1. These three kinds of existence, then, having, according to them, been now formed—one from the passion, which was matter; a second from the conversion, which was animal; and the third, that which Achamoth herself brought forth, which was spiritual.[6] Achamoth next addressed herself to the task of giving these form. But she could not succeed in doing this as respected the spiritual existence, because it was of the same nature with herself. She therefore applied herself to give form to the animal substance which had proceeded from her own conversion, and to bring forth to light the instructions of the Savior. And they say she first formed out of animal substance him who is Father and King of all things, both of these which are of the same nature with himself, that is, animal substances, which they also call right-handed, and those which sprang from the passion, and from matter, which they call left-handed. For they affirm that he formed all the things which came into existence after him, being secretly impelled thereto by his mother. From this circumstance they style him Metropator, Apator, Demiurge, and Father, saying that he is Father of the substances on the right hand, that is, of the animal, but Demiurge of those on the left, that is, of the material, while he is at the same time the king of all. For they say that this Enthymesis, desirous of making all things to the honor of the Aeons, formed images of them, or rather that the Saviour did so through her instrumentality. And she, in the image of the invisible Father, kept herself concealed from the Demiurge. But he was in the image of the only-begotten Son, and the angels and archangels created by him were in the image of the rest of the Aeons.

Book I, Chapter 9, Section 3 (329-330):

3. Learn then, you foolish men, that Jesus who suffered for us, and who dwelled among us, is Himself the Word of God.[7] For if any other of the Aeons had become flesh for our salvation, it would have been probable that the apostle spoke of another. But if the Word of the Father who descended is the same also that ascended, He, namely, the Only-begotten Son of the only God, who, according to the good pleasure of the Father, became flesh for the sake of men, the apostle certainly does not speak regarding any other, or concerning any Ogdoad,[8] but respecting our Lord Jesus Christ. For according to them, the Word did not originally become flesh. For they maintain that the Savior assumed an animal body, formed in accordance with a special dispensation by an unspeakable providence, so as to become visible and palpable. But *flesh* is that which was of old formed for Adam by God out of the dust, and it is this that John has declared the Word of God became.[9] Thus is their primary and first-begotten Ogdoad brought to nought. For, since Logos, and Monogenes, and Zoe, and Phos, and Soter, and Christus, and the Son of God, and He who became incarnate for us, have been proved to be one and the same, the Ogdoad which they have built up at once falls to pieces.[10] And when this is destroyed, their whole system sinks into ruin—a system which they falsely dream into existence. Thus they inflict injury on the Scriptures, while they build up their own hypothesis.

Book III, Chapter 11, Sections 7-8 (428-429):

7. . . . So firm is the ground upon which these Gospels rest, that the very heretics themselves bear witness to them, and, starting from these Gospels, each one of them endeavors to establish his own peculiar doctrine. For the Ebionites, who use Matthew's Gospel only, are confuted out of this very same, making false suppositions with regard to the Lord. But Marcion, mutilating that according to Luke, is proved to be a blasphemer of the only existing God, from those passages which he still retains. Those, again, who separate Jesus from Christ,

alleging that Christ remained impassible, but that it was Jesus who suffered, preferring the Gospel by Mark, if they read it with a love of truth, may have their errors rectified.)Those, moreover, who follow Valentinus, making copious use of that according to John, to illustrate their conjunctions, shall be proved to be totally in error by means of this very Gospel, as I have shown in the first book. Since, then, our opponents do bear testimony to us, and make use of these gospels, our proof derived from them is firm and true.

8. It is not possible that the Gospels can be either more or fewer in number than they are. For, since there are four zones of the world in which we live, and four principal winds, while the Church is scattered throughout all the world, and the "pillar and ground" of the Church is the Gospel and the spirit of life; it is fitting that she should have four pillars,[11] breathing out immortality on every side, and vivifying men afresh. From which fact, it is evident that the Word, the Artificer of all, He that sits upon the cherubim, and contains all things, He who was manifested to men, has given us the Gospel under four aspects, but bound together by one Spirit. . . .

## TERTULLIAN (C. 200S)

Tertullian kept quite busy refuting heretics. His writings on this score include books against Praxeas, Valentinus, and many others, as well as the three works from which selections are taken below: *On the Flesh of Christ*, *Prescription Against Heretics*, and *Against Marcion.* In this last book, Tertullian not only shows where Marcion goes wrong in his teaching of the person of Christ, but also shows us the close connection between the person of Christ and his work. In *Prescription Against the Heretics*, Tertullian lays out his version of "Rule of Faith." Early bishops in the church often wrote such rules of faith, sometimes taking the form of a creed. These rules of faith were eventually compiled as the Apostles' Creed. In *On the Flesh of*

*Christ*, Tertullian reveals the essential challenge to the biblical view of Christ in these early centuries when he summarily states, "It is his flesh that is in question."

*Tertullian, On the Flesh of Christ (De Carne Christi), Chapter 1; date: 206; source: The Ante-Nicene Fathers, Vol. III: Latin Christianity, Its Founder, Tertullian, A. Cleveland Coxe, ed. (Grand Rapids, MI: Eerdmans, 1957), 521.*

They who are so anxious to shake that belief in the resurrection which was firmly settled before the appearance of our modern Sadducees, as even to deny that the expectation thereof has any relation whatever to the flesh, have great cause for besetting the flesh of Christ also with doubtful questions, as if it either had no existence at all, or possessed a nature altogether different from human flesh. For they cannot but be apprehensive that, if it be once determined that Christ's flesh was human, a presumption would immediately arise in opposition to them, that that flesh must by all means rise again, which has already risen in Christ. Therefore we shall have to guard our belief in the resurrection from the same armory, whence they get their weapons of destruction. Let us examine our Lord's bodily substance, for about His spiritual nature all are agreed. It is His flesh that is in question.[12] Its verity and quality are the points in dispute. Did it ever exist? whence was it derived? and of what kind was it? If we succeed in demonstrating it, we shall lay down a law for our own resurrection. Marcion,[13] in order that he might deny the flesh of Christ, denied also His nativity, or else he denied His flesh in order that he might deny His nativity; because, of course, he was afraid that His nativity and His flesh bore mutual testimony to each other's reality, since there is no nativity without flesh, and no flesh without nativity. As if indeed, under the prompting of that license which is ever the same in all heresy, he too might not very well have either denied the nativity, although admitting the flesh, like Apelles, who was first a disciple of his, and afterwards an apostate, or, while admitting both the flesh and the nativity, have interpreted them in a different sense, as did Valentinus, who resembled Apelles both in his discipleship and desertion of Marcion. At all events, he who represented the flesh of Christ to be imaginary was equally able to pass off His nativity as a phantom; so that the virgin's conception, and pregnancy, and child-bearing, and then the whole course of her infant too, would have to be regarded as putative. *These facts pertaining to the nativity of Christ* would escape the notice of the same eyes and the same senses as failed to grasp the full idea of His flesh.

*Tertullian, Prescription Against the Heretics (De Praescriptione Haereticum), Chapter 13; date: 203; source: The Ante-Nicene Fathers, Vol. III, 249.*

Now, with regard to this rule of faith—that we may from this point acknowledge what it is which we defend—it is, you must know, that which prescribes the belief that there is one only God, and that He is none other than the Creator of the world, who produced all things out of nothing through His own Word, first of all sent forth; that this Word is called His Son, *and*, under the name of God, was seen "in diverse manners" by the patriarchs, heard at all times in the prophets, at last brought down by the Spirit and Power of the Father into the Virgin Mary, was made flesh in her womb, and, being born of her, went forth as Jesus Christ; thenceforth He preached the new law and the new promise of the kingdom of heaven, worked miracles; having been crucified, He rose again the third day; having ascended into the heavens, He sat at the right hand of the Father; sent instead of Himself the Power of the Holy Ghost to lead such as believe; will come with glory to take the saints to the enjoyment of everlasting life and of the heavenly promises, and to condemn the wicked to everlasting fire, after the resurrection of both these classes shall have happened, together with the restoration of their flesh. This rule, as it will be proved, was taught by Christ, and raises amongst ourselves no other questions than those which heresies introduce, and which make men heretics.

*Tertullian, Against Marcion (Contra Marcionem), Book III, Chapter 8; date: 207/208; source: The Ante-Nicene Fathers, Vol. III, 327-328.*

Our heretic must now cease to borrow poison from the Jew—"the asp," as the adage runs, "from the viper"—and henceforth vomit forth the virulence of his own disposition, as when he alleges Christ to be a phantom.[14] Except, indeed, that this opinion of his will be sure to have others to maintain it in his precocious and somewhat abortive Marcionites, whom the Apostle John designated as antichrists, when they denied that Christ was come in the flesh; not that they did this with the view of establishing the right of the other god[,] for on this point also they had been branded by the same apostle, but because they had started with assuming the incredibility of an incarnate God. Now, the more firmly the antichrist Marcion had seized this assumption, the more prepared was he, of course, to reject the bodily substance of Christ, since he had introduced his very god to our notice as neither the author nor the restorer of the flesh; and for this very reason, to be sure, as pre-eminently good, and most remote from the deceits and fallacies of the Creator. His Christ, therefore, in order to avoid all such deceits and fallacies, and the imputation, if possible, of belonging to the Creator, was not what he appeared to be, and resigned himself to be what he was not—incarnate without being flesh, human without being man, and likewise a divine Christ without being God! But why should he not have propagated also the phantom of God? Can I believe him on the subject of the internal nature, who was all wrong touching the external substance? How will it be possible to believe him true on a mystery, when he has been found so false on a plain fact? How, moreover, when he confounds the truth of the spirit with the error of the flesh, could he combine within himself that communion of light and darkness, or truth and error, which the apostle says cannot co-exist? Since, however, Christ's being flesh is now discovered to be a lie, it follows that all things which were done by the flesh of Christ were done untruly, every act of intercourse, of contact, of eating or drinking, yea, His very miracles. If with a touch, or by being touched, He freed any one of a disease, whatever was done by any corporeal act cannot be believed to have been truly done in the absence of all reality in His body itself. Nothing substantial can be allowed to have been effected by an unsubstantial thing; nothing full by a vacuity. If the habit were putative, the action was putative; if the worker were imaginary the works were imaginary. On this principle, too, the sufferings of Christ will be found not to warrant faith in Him. For He suffered nothing who did not truly suffer; and a phantom could not truly suffer. God's entire work, therefore, is subverted. Christ's death, wherein lies the whole weight and fruit of the Christian name, is denied although the apostle asserts it so expressly as undoubtedly real, making it the very foundation of the gospel, of our salvation and of his own preaching.[15] "I have delivered unto you before all things," says he, "how that Christ died for our sins, and that he was buried, and that He rose again the third day." Besides, if His flesh is denied, how is His death to be asserted; for death is the proper suffering of the flesh, which returns through death back to the earth out of which it was taken, according to the law of its Maker? Now, if His death be denied, because of the denial of His flesh, there will be no certainty of His resurrection. For He rose not, for the very same reason that He died not, even because He possessed not the reality of the flesh, to which as death accrues, so does resurrection likewise. Similarly, if Christ's resurrection be nullified, ours also is destroyed. If Christ's *resurrection* be not realized, neither shall that be for which Christ came. For just as they, who said that there is no resurrection of the dead, are refuted by the apostle from the resurrection of Christ, so, if the resurrection of Christ falls to the ground, the resurrection of the dead is also swept away. And so our faith is vain, and vain also is the preaching of the apostles. Moreover, they even show themselves to be false witnesses of God, because they testified that He raised up Christ, whom He did not raise. And we remain in our sins still. And those who have slept in Christ have perished; destined, forsooth, to rise again, but peradventure in a phantom state, just like Christ.

## HIPPOLYTUS (C. 170-C. 236)

In his ambitiously titled work *Refutation of All Heresies*, Hippolytus very nearly accomplishes what he proposes to do. The book largely consists of concise descriptions of the well-known and obscure heretics. He spends considerable time on Marcion and Valentinus. Concerning Valentinus, Hippolytus rightly accuses him of plagiarizing Plato, arguing quite well that Valentinus merely copied the great Greek philosopher's ideas (Book VI, Chapters 16, 24). To conclude this work, Hippolytus first recaps his trek through the heresies and then offers his understanding of the true doctrine of Christ (Book X, Chapters 29-30).

*Hippolytus, Refutation of All Heresies (Refutatio Omnium Haeresium), Book VI, Chapters 16, 24; date: c. 222; source: The Ante-Nicene Fathers, Vol. V: The Writings of the Fathers Down to A.D. 325, A. Cleveland Coxe, ed. (Grand Rapids, MI: Eerdmans, 1957), 81-82, 85.*

Chapter 16: The heresy of Valentinus is certainly, then, connected with the Pythagorean and Platonic theory. For Plato, in the Timaeus, altogether derives his impressions from Pythagoras, and therefore Timaeus himself is his Pythagorean stranger. Wherefore, it appears expedient that we should commence by reminding the reader of a few points of the Pythagorean and Platonic theory, and that then we should proceed to declare the opinions of Valentinus. For even though in the books previously finished by us with so much pains are contained the opinions advanced by both Pythagoras and Plato, yet at all events I shall not be acting unreasonably, in now also calling to the recollection of the reader, by means of an epitome, the principal heads of the favorite tenets of these speculative philosophers. And this recapitulation will facilitate our knowledge of the doctrines of Valentinus, by means of a nearer comparison, and by similarity of composition of the two systems. For Pythagoras and Plato derived these tenets originally from the Egyptians, and introduced their novel opinions among the Greeks. But Valentinus took his opinions from these, because, although he has suppressed the truth regarding his obligations to the Greek philosophers, and in this way has endeavored to construct a doctrine, peculiarly his own, yet, in point of fact, he has altered the doctrines of those thinkers in names only, and numbers, and has adopted a peculiar terminology of his own. Valentinus has formed his definitions by measures, in order that he may establish an Hellenic heresy, diversified no doubt, but unstable, and not connected with Christ. . . .

Chapter 24: Of some such nature, as I who have accurately examined their systems have attempted to state compendiously, is the opinion of Pythagoras and Plato. And from this system, not from the Gospels, Valentinus, as we have proved, has collected the materials of heresy—I mean his own heresy—and may therefore justly be reckoned a Pythagorean and Platonist, not a Christian. Valentinus, therefore, and Heracleon, and Ptolemaeus, and the entire school of these heretics, as disciples of Pythagoras and Plato, and following these guides, have laid down as the fundamental principle of their doctrine the arithmetical system. For, likewise, according to these Valentinians, the originating cause of the universe is a Monad, unbegotten, imperishable, incomprehensible, inconceivable, productive, and a cause of the generation of all existent things. And the aforesaid Monad is styled by them Father.[16]

*Refutation of All Heresies, Book X, Chapters 29-30, The Ante-Nicene Fathers, Vol. V, 152-153.*

Chapter 29: . . . This Logos the Father in the latter days sent forth, no longer to speak by a prophet, and not wishing that *the* Word, being obscurely proclaimed, should be made the subject of mere conjecture, but that He should be manifested, so that we could see Him with our own eyes.[17] This *Logos*, I say, the Father sent forth, in order that the world, on beholding Him, might reverence Him who was delivering precepts not by the person of prophets, nor terrifying the soul by an angel, but who was Himself—He that had spoken—corporally present amongst us. This *Logos* we know to have received a body from a virgin, and to have remodeled the old man by a new creation. And we believe the *Logos* to have passed through every period in this life, in order that He Himself might serve as a law for every age, and that, by being present amongst us, He might exhibit His own manhood as an aim for all men. And that by Himself in person He might prove that God made nothing evil, and that man possesses the capacity of self-determination, inasmuch as he is able to will and not to will, and is endued with power to do both. This Man we know to have been made out of the compound of our humanity. For if He were not of the same nature with ourselves, in vain does He ordain that we should imitate the Teacher. For if that Man happened to be of a different substance from us, why does He lay injunctions similar to those He has received on myself, who am born weak; and how is this the act of one that is good and just? In order, however, that He might not be supposed to be different from us, He even underwent toil, and was willing to endure hunger, and did not refuse to feel thirst, and sunk into the quietude of slumber. He did not protest against His Passion, but became obedient unto death, and manifested His resurrection. Now in all these acts He offered up, as the first-fruits, His own manhood, in order that thou, when thou art in tribulation, may not be disheartened, but, confessing thyself to be a man of like nature with the Redeemer, may dwell in expectation of also receiving what the Father has granted unto this Son.

Chapter 30: Such is the true doctrine in regard of the divine nature, O you men, Greeks and Barbarians, Chaldeans and

Assyrians, Egyptians and Libyans, Indians and Ethiopians, Celts, and ye Latins, who lead armies, and all ye that inhabit Europe, and Asia, and Libya. And to you I am become an adviser, inasmuch as I am a disciple of the benevolent Logos, and hence humane, in order that you may hasten and by us may be taught who the true God is, and what is His well-ordered creation. Do not devote your attention to the fallacies of artificial discourses, nor the vain promises of plagiarizing heretics, but to the venerable simplicity of unassuming truth. And by means of this knowledge you shall escape the approaching threat of the fire of judgment, and the rayless scenery of gloomy Tartarus, where never shines a beam from the irradiating voice of the Word!

## CHAPTER THREE

# The Triumph of Athanasius: The Battle for Christ at Nicea

*We believe . . . in one Lord Jesus Christ, the only begotten Son of God, begotten of his Father before all worlds, God of God, Light of Light, very God of very God, begotten not made, being of one substance with the Father.*

**THE NICENE CREED**

*But Athanasius, after being engaged in so many and such severe conflicts on behalf of the church, departed this life . . . having governed that church [of Alexandria] amidst the greatest perils for forty-six years.*

**SOCRATES, *CHURCH HISTORY***

**P**rior to *The Da Vinci Code*, you would have been hard-pressed to find many conversant with the Nicene Creed. But now nearly fifty million readers, not to mention masses of moviegoers, know a thing or two about it. Chapter 55 fills them in, as the dashing Teabing enlightens Sophie:

> "Indeed," Teabing said. "Stay with me. During this fusion of religions, Constantine needed to strengthen the new Christian tradition, and held a famous ecumenical gathering known as the council of Nicea." . . .
>
> "My dear," Teabing declared, "until *that* moment in history, Jesus was viewed by his followers as a mortal prophet . . . a great and powerful man, but a *man* nonetheless. A mortal."

Sophie, apparently stunned at this revelation, stammers, "Not the Son of God?" To which Teabing replies, "Right . . . Jesus' establishment as 'the Son of God' was officially proposed and voted on by the Council of Nicea." Now Sophie is flabbergasted: "Hold on. You're saying Jesus' divinity was the result of a *vote*?" Then Dan Brown has his character put the exclamation point on the matter: "A relatively close vote at that." As Sophie "glances" at Langdon, he offers his "soft nod of concurrence."

## THE SEVEN ECUMENICAL COUNCILS

| Council | Date | Issue |
| --- | --- | --- |
| 1. Nicea | 325 | Deity of Christ; opposed to Arianism |
| 2. Constantinople I | 381 | Deity of Christ; opposed to Arianism |
| 3. Ephesus | 431 | Two-nature Christology; opposed to Apollinarianism |
| 4. Chalcedon | 451 | Two-nature Christology; opposed to Apollinarianism, Nestorianism, and Eutychianism |
| 5. Constantinople II | 553 | Two-nature Christology; opposed to monophysitism |
| 6. Constantinople III | 680 | Two-nature Christology; opposed to monotheletism |
| 7. Nicea II | 787 | Icons |

The Roman Catholic Church continues to convene councils, the last being Vatican II, 1962–1965. Since the split of the Roman Catholic Church (the so-called "Western Church") from Greek Orthodoxy (the so-called "Eastern Church") in 1054, these councils are not considered "ecumenical" since each side refuses to recognize the other. Prior to the split, seven councils were held. Some claim there was an eighth council, Constantinople IV in 870. The councils produced creeds and reams of canons, specific teachings on a variety of issues. In addition to these seven or eight councils, numerous synods and official gatherings of the church were held. The rulings of these councils and synods and the later medieval councils, as well as the teachings of the popes, constitute Canon Law, or church law, for Roman Catholicism. Protestants tend only to look to the Creeds from Nicea (325) and Chalcedon (451).

Later, once Teabing is "talking faster," he further adds that "because Constantine upgraded Jesus' status almost four centuries *after* Jesus' death," a whole new canon of Scripture was necessary. Constantine, according to Brown's Teabing, commissioned a new Bible, squelching those gospels that portrayed Christ's humanity and "embellished those gospels that made him godlike."[1]

First, we see Brown's problem with math—from A.D. 30 or so to 325 may span four centuries, but it is actually just shy of three hundred years. But Brown has many more problems beyond simple subtraction. Sticking with numbers, the vote at Nicea was *not* close. Pinpointing the number of bishops in attendance is difficult. Numbers range from 220 to 318. The number of yea votes ranged anywhere from 218 to 316. Scholars know the number of nay votes with accuracy. There were two, cast by friends of Arius. "Close" it most certainly was not. Further, while accomplished militarily and politically, ascribing to Constantine such sophisticated ecclesiastical and theological triumphs is a bit of a stretch. The most significant problem, however, with Brown's dialogue in Chapter 55 is that it is plainly, categorically, and blatantly wrong. As our look into the first three centuries in Chapter 1 revealed, the early church fathers often and strongly affirmed the deity of Christ.[2]

The only silver lining in Dan Brown's blockbuster novel is that at least people are hearing and talking about what happened at Nicea in 325. While not *establishing* the divinity of Christ, Nicea did *express* his deity, and his humanity for that matter, with clarity and eloquence and with a finality that has stood the test of time, providing the church with the orthodox definition of the person of Christ. The Nicene Creed, however, came at a cost. While the vote was not close, even by any stretch of a novelist's imagination, it nevertheless sparked a controversy that spanned most of the fourth century. This chapter explores this struggle and the Council of Nicea in 325, where it all began. Like a classic western, the story of Nicea has its good guys and bad. Wearing the white hat is Athanasius, while on the other side is Arius. This story even has its bad sheriff, with Constantius II playing the part.

## THE NICENE COUNCIL

The name has changed, but the city remains. Today Nicea is known as Iznik, nestled along the shores of Lake Iznik, not many miles south of Istanbul (formerly Constantinople). Tourists travel there today to see the Roman ruins, attracted to the walls built in the fourth century that surrounded the city, standing nearly thirty feet high, and attracted to the ruins of the Church of Hagia Sophia, site of the seventh ecumenical council in 787. It is a small city of immense beauty, stretched out on a fertile plain bordered by Lake Iznik and by mountains. In 325 well over two hundred bishops gathered at this lakeside resort at the request of Constantine to settle the percolating controversy over the teachings of Arius (250–336), a presbyter from Alexandria. The bulk of the bishops came from points east, Arius's region. Among them was the young but formidable and tenacious Athanasius (297–373), the recently appointed bishop of Alexandria.

Numerous issues filled the Nicene Council's agenda: the date of Easter and the occasion best to celebrate it; procedural issues such as the electing of bishops and elders; the jurisdiction of bishops; and the administration of the sacraments. The question of the person of Christ, however, dominated the discussions that took place during the months of May to July 325. Both the issue itself and the way in which the church handled it could not be more crucial. This was the first church-wide council, which is why it's called an *ecumenical* council. The bishops were the participants, but the elders and the laity of the church were watching, not to mention Emperor Constantine and a host of government officials. The talk in the street across the empire was of Nicea.[3]

Behind the commotion stood Arius. He taught, in a rather sophisticated manner, that there was a time when Christ was not. He denied his eternality, instead viewing Christ as created or made by God as the first being. Christ then created or made everything else. This led Arius to view Christ as more than human, but not as identical in essence or being to God. Instead Arius viewed Christ as *similar* in essence to God. He used the Greek word *homoiousion*. This is a compound word from the word *homoi*, meaning "similar," and the word *ousion*, meaning "substance" or "essence." Substance or essence means, in this case, that which constitutes or makes a thing or a person what that thing or person is. Now we are wading in deep and murky waters. Let me try to help us get a better handle on what's going on in this discussion.

The substance or essence of you is what makes you *you*. Without it, you wouldn't be *you* anymore. Substance or essence isn't, at least in this case, physical. I am physically quite different now than two months before I was born or when I was two months old, two years old, or even twenty years old. Yet all along I have been of the same essence. I have been *I* every step of the way. So it is with you. Your essence is what makes you *you*, and my essence is what makes me *I*.

Now to return to Arius. He said that which makes God *God* is not what Christ *is*. God and Christ are not of identical essence; Jesus is merely of similar (*homoi*) essence (*ousion*). Arius further held his teaching to be true to Scripture. First, he held that God created or made Christ on the basis of Paul's reference to Christ as "the firstborn of all creation" (Col. 1:15). Arius also understood the reference to Christ as the "only begotten" in John 3:16 as teaching that Christ came into existence, that he was made, and that he had not existed for all eternity. Arius further relied on Deuteronomy 6:4: "Hear, O Israel: The LORD our God, the LORD is one." Arius rejected the notion of the Trinity, that God is one in essence and three in persons. And he rejected the deity of Christ. To be sure, Arius had a high view, a very high view, of Christ, but his view fell short. Writing many centuries after Arius and in a different context, J. Gresham Machen made this stinging condemnation of a similarly faulty view of Christ, exclaiming, "The next thing less than the infinite is infinitely less." Arius's Christ of similar essence or substance to the Father is ultimately infinitely less than the Christ who is of the same essence or substance of the Father.[4]

Those familiar with the views of the Jehovah's Witnesses recognize immediately the connection to Arius. In fact, Arianism has made numerous appearances throughout history since the 300s. As we saw in Chapter 1, the term *docetism* functioned both to refer to specific heresies and to more general tendencies to deny the full and literal humanity of Christ. The term *Arianism* functions in the same way. It refers both to the specific fourth-century heresy of the bishop Arius and also to the general tendency to deny the full deity of Christ. And docetists and Arians we will have with us always.

## THE EXILED BISHOP

Arius, prolific and sophisticated, met his match in Athanasius. Athanasius was the younger of the two and far outlived Arius. (Part of the moral of this story is to pick older opponents.) There is some debate over the official role of Athanasius at Nicea in 325. If his accepted birth date of 297 holds true, then he was technically too young to be a bishop. Playing off the understanding that Christ began his public ministry at age thirty, bishops could not be elected to their post until they reached that age. His age notwithstanding and official roles aside, Athanasius made an enormous contribution to the council, though it consisted of only one word. Actually his contribution consisted of one letter. To be technically accurate, his contribution consisted of *striking* one letter.

## IT'S ALL GREEK TO ME

Getting a handle on the terms used by theologians in the fourth century is crucial to understanding the controversy. This chart provides an overview.

| Greek Word | Meaning | Proponent |
|---|---|---|
| *Homoousias*<br>*homo* = same<br>*ousias* = substance | same substance/essence | Athanasius |
| *Homoiousias*<br>*homoi* = similar | similar substance/essence | Arius |
| *Heteroousias*<br>*hetero* = different | different substance/essence | Eunomius |

Arius had considered Christ to be of similar substance to the Father, using the Greek word *homoiousion* (*homoi* meaning "similar" and *ousion* meaning "substance"). Athanasius instead summarized the biblical teaching on Christ's deity by using the Greek word *homoousion*. This word first surfaced around the 260s in response to refuting the heretical teaching of Paul of Samasota, as discussed in Chapter 1. This, too, is a compound word—*homo* meaning "same" or "identical" and *ousion* meaning "essence" or "substance." Jesus is of one substance or essence with the Father. He is fully divine; as the Nicene Creed puts it, "very God of very God."

Athanasius was applying the work of Tertullian, who coined the term *Trinity* to address the specific issue of Christ's identity. Tertullian defined the Trinity as three persons in one essence, thus capturing in a systematic expression great strands of biblical teaching on the oneness of God and the three distinct yet equal persons of the Father, Son, and Holy Spirit. Athanasius applied the term "essence" (*ousion*) and the meaning the term conveys to the person of Christ. Christ is of the same or identical essence with the Father. Yet Christ also exists as a separate person, distinct in his own identity as Christ the Son. The bishops at Nicea did not vote Christ into deity, and neither did Constantine "upgrade" Jesus' status from being a mere mortal to being divine, Dan Brown's musings aside. The Council at Nicea with Athanasius leading the way did, however, express the biblical teaching clearly and succinctly. Christ is God, they said. And they further said that any who held otherwise stood condemned as a heretic.

In addition to clearly and forcefully articulating the deity of Christ, the Nicene Creed also laid great stress on the humanity of Christ. The creed holds that Christ was begotten, not made as Arius held. Christ came down from heaven, was incarnate, was virgin-born. He lived, he suffered, and he died on a cross—the ultimate testimony to his humanity. Then he rose again and ascended into heaven, the God-man who will return someday to judge the world.

### THE CONVERSION OF CONSTANTINE

One of the most enigmatic figures in church history is the Roman Emperor Constantine. And his so-called conversion to Christianity ranks among the most contested of events. Eusebius, the early church historian, praised Constantine, writing a glowing, if not hagiographic, biography. Others in the early church lined up as well to sing his praises and extol his Christian virtues. Other contemporaries, as well as many historians, aren't quite as sure. Constantine secured his power at the Battle of Milvian Bridge by defeating Maxentius, known to history as Maxentius the Usurper. Constantine credited God for the victory. Prior to the battle he had a vision in which God gave him a sign, informing him that by this sign he would have victory. The sign (☧) consisted of an arrangement of the Greek letters *chi*, transliterated as *ch* in English, and *rho*, transliterated as *r* in English. These are the first two letters in the word *Christ*. In gratitude for the victory, Constantine issued a series of edicts legalizing and then granting favorable status to Christianity. He then convened the Nicene Council. Yet there are some ambiguities and perplexities. He seemed to hold on to many of his old pagan traditions and rituals, and he was not baptized as a Christian until his deathbed.

As the council voted and came to a close, it was quite clear that Arius was in the unenviable position of the minority, a minority of himself and two bishops. His view was condemned, and he was a heretic. Arius, however, was a popular teacher, and he was quite savvy. He had even managed to turn his views into catchy songs and jingles for worship. Among some of the laity, Arius's views made sense, and they relied on his (mis)understanding of texts like Colossians 1:15 and his (mis)use of Deuteronomy 6:4. Condemning Arius at the Council of Nicea was relatively easy compared to the task of rooting out Arian teachings from the church. Things got more complex as Constantine's power waned and his son Constantius II's power waxed.

Constantine, who ruled in the west from 307–324 and over a united empire from 324–337, knew that his strengths were not in the realm of theology. He was a politician and a general. And as a politician he could see what havoc the Arian controversy caused in the church and what it threatened to do in his united empire. For decades he had waged wars; he wasn't about to let a theological dispute upset the peace he now enjoyed. Consequently he called and funded the council, but he left it to the theologians and bishops to do the council's work and to carry out its decisions. He did send Athanasius on his first exile in 336, but that came after he apparently grew tired of the harping and nagging of other bishops who disliked Athanasius, not sharing his zeal for orthodox doctrine. Yet Constantine tended to let the church run itself.

Not so with the son. Constantius II initially shared power with his brothers Constantine II and Constans—not a great deal of originality going on here in the naming. But from 337–361 Constantius II had control of the Eastern Empire, which encompassed Alexandria. He held control of a united empire from 353–361. Constantius II favored Arius. After Arius's death in 337, Constantius II favored those bishops who, despite voting against him in 325, might now support his ideas. The year 337 also witnessed the passing of Constantine—a baptized Christian on his deathbed. As Constantius II assumed power, he set his sights on Athanasius. Constantius II wasted no time, sending Athanasius into a seven-year exile beginning in 339.

Even though Athanasius was on the right side of the line between heresy and orthodoxy, and even though he enjoyed overwhelming support throughout the church, Constantius II saw to it that Athanasius would have his troubles. Sensing that Arianism had not been rooted out of the church, Athanasius applied the bulk of his energies to making sure that what the council decided at Nicea in 325 would stand and be the only accepted teaching in the churches. He used his pulpit to preach sermons on the orthodox view, directly and vehemently condemning the teachings of Arius. He used his skill with words to write letter after letter on the issue, as well as major treatises such as *On the Incarnation* (335 or 336). And whenever Athanasius's crusade against Arianism was gaining traction, Constantius II stepped in. He would dispatch some troops to have Athanasius exiled—one time Athanasius was carried away during a Communion service. When the public and clerical outcry grew too large for Constantius II to ignore, he would reluctantly let Athanasius return to his post as bishop. As Athanasius returned to his mission of proclaiming the orthodox view of Christ, Constantius II would dispatch the troops again. Athanasius endured five exiles in all: one by Constantine (336–338), two by Constantius II (339–346 and 356–362), one by Julian (362–364), and one by Valens (365–366). In fact, Athanasius spent nearly as much time in exile from his post as he did in it.

Athanasius contended with much more than exiles. Constantius II geared up a campaign aimed at smearing Athanasius's reputation. He coerced other bishops to join him in condemning Athanasius. Constantius II treated his own brothers no less kindly. In 350 he forced the suicide of Constans, one of his brothers and a co-regent in the Western Empire, opening the way for himself to assume rule of a united empire in 353. Constantius II's reign is full of such intrigue and treachery.

At one point, in the spirit of ecumenicity, Constantius II was able to strong-arm all of the bishops into signing a document against Athanasius. It sparked a new slogan: *Athanasius contra mundum*, "Athanasius against the world." Indeed Athanasius contended with the world, both the world of the church and the world of politics.

Even during the exiles Athanasius managed to have the upper hand. These exiles were not idle times. In fact, Athanasius used the time to write his major treatises. In addition to his theological works, he also wrote a biography of Antony. Antony had fled into the deserts of Egypt to escape persecution, establishing one of the earliest monasteries, or at least the precursor to the monasteries that would be so prevalent in the medieval era. Athanasius was so impressed with Antony's spirituality and commitment to Christ that he wanted to tell his story to inspire others. Athanasius's *Life of Antony* had many readers in the early church, not the least of which was Augustine. Next to the Bible, Augustine credits Athanasius's *Life of Antony* as having the most significant impact on his life.

It was also while exiled that Athanasius correlated his thoughts on the person of Christ in his book *On the Incarnation*. Ironically, the popularity of that book, written during an exile, triggered yet another time of exile for Athanasius. While Athanasius's opponent was the theologian Arius, his true nemesis was Emperor Constantius II. Through it all and against the world, however, Athanasius persevered. A good theologian with a brilliant mind and a persuasive manner, he also possessed the singular character trait of tenacity. Athanasius took hold of an idea, the word *homoousion*, and would not for life or limb or exile let go.[5]

You might have heard someone refer to theologians as wasting time and energy in their ivory-tower debates. (In the interest of full disclosure, I for one have never lived or worked in an ivory tower, and I can't say I ever met a fellow theologian who has.) This *ivory tower* expression reflects the sentiment of those who easily grow weary of apparently inane theological debate and the seemingly endless wrestling over views on peripheral matters. Indeed, to the making of theological views on any and all subjects there appears to be no end. Yet the church could not be as grateful to anyone as they can and should be to Athanasius, a theologian who wrangled over not just a word but over a letter for six decades! Athanasius spent his life in one long theological debate over apparent minutiae. And if he hadn't, we'd all be in trouble.

## FOR US AND FOR OUR SALVATION

Athanasius's tenacity paid off. After his death in 373, the second ecumenical council convened at Constantinople in 381. Constantius II had long passed from the scene, and Theodosius II, who ruled over the Eastern Empire from 379–395, was anxious to rout the Arian controversy. At Constantinople II any potential nod to Arianism, or even a wink to it, was put out of the church once and for all. Athanasius's view of Christ as being of one substance or essence (*homoousion*) with the Father won the day, while Arius's view of Christ as similar substance with the Father (*homoiousion*) was declared to be outside the bounds of orthodoxy and thus condemned.

One has to ask why Athanasius endured so much for so long. Why did he wrangle for decades over one word, over one letter, *i*? The reason comes in a phrase also found in the Nicene Creed, a phrase that is attributed to Athanasius. It may not be too much of a stretch to claim this phrase to be one of the most profound, if not beautiful, phrases in all of theological literature, the phrase "*for us and for our salvation.*" Athanasius wrangled with the best minds of the day and endured persecution at the hands of the most powerful politicians of the day, all for the sake of the gospel. The *person* of Christ, Athanasius believed, had everything to do with the *work* of Christ. If the church got it wrong on the person of Christ, the church would be wrong on the work of Christ. Athanasius spent six decades contending for a letter and contending against the world for the sake of the gospel.

## ATHANASIUS'S ALLIES

While *Athanasius contra mundum* appeared to be true, in reality he did not stand alone. The so-called Cappadocian Fathers rank chief among his allies in the struggle for the orthodox view of Christ. These three stalwarts of the early church include the two brothers Basil of Caesarea (329–379) and Gregory of Nyssa (335–395), along with Gregory of Nazianzus (329–390). They were bishops in those three cities. It was Gregory of Nyssa who led the charge in firmly establishing the view of Athanasius at the Council of Constantinople in 381. Yet all three of them worked tirelessly, mainly through sermons and writings, to help the church think through the biblical teaching on the doctrine of the Trinity and the doctrine of Christ.

Cappadocia was a barren region in Asia Minor, just above Paul's hometown of Tarsus. According to Acts 2:9, Cappadocians were present at the day of Pentecost. Not much is known of how the church there fared from its beginnings until 250 or so. At that time Gregory Thaumaturgus, which translated means "wonder-worker," made his way into Cappadocia and firmly established a church. One of his early converts was the grandmother of Gregory of Nyssa and Basil of Caesarea. Anthony Meredith, in his recent biography of Gregory of Nyssa, notes, "The family was distinguished and propertied, Christian and cultivated."[6] While studying at Athens, Basil struck a friendship with Gregory of Nazianzus. When Basil returned home, he lived as a hermit on his family's land. He put his education to use as he began writing treatises on the Arian controversy. His sharp wit caught the attention of the bishops and clergy. Basil was plucked from his life of seclusion and began his work in the church, being primed for the bishopric of Caesarea, Cappadocia's capital city. Basil assumed the post in 372.

The next year, with the passing of Athanasius, the mantle of leadership of the orthodox bishops in the east fell to Basil. He wrote many sermons and homilies, as well as one significant treatise, *On the Holy Spirit*, in which he developed the doctrine of the Trinity. He also left his mark on the church through his work as bishop. He arranged for his old university mate Gregory to be appointed bishop of Nazianzus and he arranged for his brother Gregory to be appointed bishop of Nyssa. The three cities formed a triangle in Cappadocia. Their influence, however, extended far beyond the region of Cappadocia and far beyond their own lives. In fact, their work impacted theology throughout the church for centuries after their death.

Gregory of Nyssa was appointed bishop in 372, one of the first things his brother Basil had arranged in his post as bishop. He did not share in his brother's university education at Athens, being educated at home instead. He proved, however, no less formidable intellectually. His treatise, rather directly titled *That We Should Not Think of Saying There are Three Gods*, also moved the church along in its orthodox formulation and expression of the Trinity. What we see in this work, as well as in the works of the other two Cappadocian Fathers, is that the controversy over Arius had developed beyond the sole issue of the deity of Christ and had by now encompassed the way the church understood God the Father, Jesus the Son, and the Holy Spirit—the three persons in one. The language these theologians gave us has remained the orthodox definition of the Trinity. They used the Greek word *ousia*, meaning "substance" or "essence," to speak of the oneness of God and the word *hypostasis*, meaning "person," to speak of the three persons or three members of the Trinity. This expression—one substance, three persons—is a way of capturing both the unity and oneness of God and the individual identities of the three persons. We use the word *Trinity*, which comes into the English language as a transliterated Latin word, to express this phrase in one succinct word.

Gregory of Nyssa also wrote a work directly aimed at the Arian controversy entitled *Against Eunomius*. Eunomius, the bishop of Cyzicus, was a leading player among what historians have called "the Arian clique." In fact, Eunomius took Arianism to radical extremes, moving beyond the idea that Christ is of a similar substance, *homoiousias*, and positing that the Father and Son must be of entirely different substances. The word to express this is *heteroousias*, a compound word made from *hetero*, meaning "different," and *ousias*, meaning "substance." Arianism was spinning out of control.

When Theodosius I became emperor in the east, he realized the need for a council to address the problem of Arius, to finish what the Council of Nicea had started about six decades prior. In 381 he called for a council at the capital city of Constantinople (modern-day Istanbul). Gregory of Nazianzus, the other Cappadocian Father, presided over the council. Gregory of Nazianzus's contribution to theology came through his many and sometimes rather lengthy letters, orations, and even poems. Gregory of Nazianzus held the same post as his father before him. He took it, however, reluctantly. Like Basil, he would have preferred the quiet life of the scholar, but, again like Basil, he found himself pressed into service in the ecclesiastical hierarchy. Both he and Basil had made a pact at Athens: they would commit their lives to being philosophers. In a letter to Basil, Gregory confesses, "I have failed to keep my promise . . . not of my own will, but because one law prevailed against another; I mean the law which bids us honor our parents."[7]

Gregory, however, was primed for the post through his Christian upbringing—by his own account, his mother led his father to conversion—his university training, and his dogged commitment to orthodoxy. His prowess at theology accounts for how he is known, in addition to Gregory of Nazianzus, as simply Gregory the Theologian. He also lacked fear. At Athens one of his fellow classmates was Julian, who would later become emperor in the west and who was even then spouting his pagan beliefs that would come to earn him the title Julian the Apostate. Gregory of Nazianzus did not flinch in confronting him. All of this made him more than suitable for overseeing the Council at Constantinople, and in that position he made sure that Athanasius's view would prevail. It would be a victory, however, that Athanasius missed, for he died eight years prior to the council that would vindicate him and his lifelong commitment to *homoousias*. But Athanasius's decades of perseverance paid off. The church would fully and truly affirm that Christ is of the same substance as God the Father. And they would further affirm that was the exclusive way to speak of Christ.[8]

The three Cappadocian Fathers were comrades and even brothers in arms—theological arms, that is. In one of his letters to Basil, Gregory of Nazianzus, on the occasion of Basil's ordination as a priest and in reflection of his own position, observes again their mutual reluctance. But he quickly adds, "Since it has come about, we must bear it, at least so it seems clear to me; and especially when we take the times into consideration, which are bringing in upon us so many heretical tongues." On yet another occasion he writes, "It is a time for prudence and endurance, and that we should not let anyone appear to be of higher courage than ourselves, or let all our labors and toils be in an instant brought to nothing." Their courage did not flag as they found strength and support in each other.[9]

I suspect most Christians today would not be able to name the three Cappadocian Fathers, but the church owes these three much gratitude nevertheless. The two Gregorys and Basil would have preferred a life of obscurity, spending their days turning over philosophical conundrums in their own heads and relishing their quiet pursuit of God. Instead they formed a phalanx of gifted, prudent, and courageous theologians defending orthodoxy on the front lines. And they came at a precarious time in the life of the church. Their main opposition did not stem from the ecclesiastical authorities as much as it stemmed from the emperors pulling the strings behind the scenes. They contended with Julian the Apostate and the other emperors who tilted toward Arianism. They would find their political ally in Theodosius. While Theodosius lived, the orthodox bishops couldn't speak highly enough of him. And when he died, they took their rhetoric even higher.

## "THE AIR WAS SHUDDERING IN UNBROKEN GLOOM"

When he wanted to, Ambrose, bishop of Milan, could turn on the rhetoric. It was his preaching, in part, that caused Augustine to give Christianity some consideration. Augustine had thought the Bible, and the theologians and pastors who proclaimed it, to be less than rhetorically impressive. Then he heard Ambrose preach at Milan. Ambrose had been a provincial governor before he donned the bishop's robe. Theodosius died in 395, during his bishopric, and Ambrose gave a funeral oration not lacking in length or in ornamentation. He started by observing the severe weather, verging on apocalyptic, that had been occurring throughout the empire, a sure sign that a great man was passing from this earth. "The air was shuddering in unbroken gloom," Ambrose observed, adding, "the earth was shaken by tremors and filled with floods of waters." He continued, "Why should not the universe itself bemoan the fact that this prince was presently to be snatched away?" Indeed, after the ambiguities of Constantine, the wranglings of Constantius II, the pagan apostasy of Julian, the deeply orthodox and pious Theodosius I was greatly welcomed and would now be sorely missed. Ambrose may have overindulged his rhetorical abilities in the eulogy but, all things considered, not by much.[10]

The church mingled with the empire throughout the fourth century, as it would in the next, and for the millennium after that. The church began the century on the run, facing one of the most dire persecutions by Diocletian, emperor in the East from 286–305. Eusebius, bishop of Caesarea and one of the earliest church historians, records that the jails were so full of Christians that there was no room for true criminals, triggering a crime spree. After him followed Constantine and the great reversal. Of Constantine's rise to power, Eusebius asserts, "Thus then the God of all, the Supreme Governor of the whole universe, by his own will appointed Constantine." Christianity was made a legal religion by Constantine's Edict of Milan in 313. Christianity would quickly become the favored religion of the empire. Eusebius experienced both worlds of want and of plenty. As he looked around the Council of Nicea in 325, he saw fellow bishops who had been jailed for their faith, some even having visible scars from the persecutions they had endured. Now they sat in a great council, enjoying feasts provided by the emperor himself.[11]

## ROMAN EMPERORS OF THE FOURTH CENTURY

| West | East | Church Councils |
|------|------|-----------------|
| Constantine I 307–324 | Licinius 308–324 | |
| United Constantius 324–337 | | Nicea 325 |
| West | East | |
| Constantine II 337–340 | Constantius II 337–353 | |
| Constans 337–350 | | |
| Magnetius 350–353 | | |
| United Constantius II 353–361 | | |
| Julian 361–363 | | |
| Jovian 363–364 | | |
| West | East | |
| Valentinian I 364–375 | Valens 364–378 | |
| Gratian 375–383 | Procopius 365–366 | |
| Valentinian II 375–392 | Theodosius I 375–395 | Constantinople I, 381 |

As Constantine aged, his sons began vying for power. Constantius II, who favored Arius, controlled the east, while Constans, who favored Athanasius, had shared power in the west. Constans once threatened war against his brother in an attempt to get Athanasius released from exile. But Constantius II held the upper hand, the great weight of which was felt by Constans and Athanasius and all those on the side of orthodoxy.

Once Constantius II died, things weren't automatically better. Julian assumed the throne of a united empire from 361–363. He's not called Julian the Apostate for nothing. He did not share in the empire's turn toward Jerusalem. Instead he reverted back to the old pagan gods of earlier centuries. He tolerated the church and its bishops as long as they steered clear of preaching the exclusivity of the Christian faith. Athanasius ran afoul of Julian when he had a hard time steering clear of such preaching. When Julian's brief reign ended, a series of Arian emperors ascended the thrones of what had once again become a divided empire. And then came Theodosius I. Now we can see some justification for Ambrose's flights of rhetoric. The church had existed for the first three hundred years in a hostile relationship with the empire. It was learning, throughout the fourth century, how to live with its freedom. Regardless of the assessment one makes of the impact of this union of church and state, one thing  should at least be clear: the church of the ages was given the Nicene Creed and finalized and formalized it at Constantinople, and the emperors picked up the tab.

## CONCLUSION

At the beginning of this chapter I mentioned that the story of Christological developments in the fourth century has all the trappings of a classic western. We have the good guys and the bad, roles played by theologians and politicians alike. But the stakes are much higher than the sheer exhilaration brought about when good triumphs over evil. The gospel, as Athanasius so compellingly argued, was at stake. Arius's Jesus, falling even a scintilla short of deity, is not the Jesus of the Bible, nor is he the Jesus of salvation.

The Councils at Nicea (325) and Constantinople (381) emphatically affirmed the divine and human natures of Christ.

The Nicene Creed declares Christ's deity—he is "very God of very God"—and Christ's humanity—"he was made man." The Creed further and rather eloquently declares that this view of the person of Christ has everything to do with the work of Christ. He is the God-man *for us and for our salvation*."

The affirmations of the deity and humanity of Christ, however, opened the door for a whole new set of problems for theologians as they attempted to state in precise language, true to Scripture, how these two natures relate and coexist in one person, Christ. These problems dominated the fourth century and the great church council occurring in the middle of it, the Council of Chalcedon. And there, too, new good guys and bad guys would emerge.

## CHAPTER FOUR

# In Their Own Words:
## Select Documents from the
## Fourth Century

Theology, personalities, and politics. These ingredients resulted
in the controversy over the person of Christ that erupted at the
Council of Nicea (325) and dominated the fourth century. This
chapter offers a sampling of the primary texts of this drama.
Beginning with Eusebius's praise of Constantine, we see that
the Christological developments in the 300s must be set against
the backdrop of the emperors. Eusebius and the other bishops
endured an intense season of persecution at the beginning of the
300s. Constantine ushered in a welcome wave of relief. While
the persecution ebbed, however, the doctrinal controversy was
just beginning to flow.

Arius's view that Christ was created and not eternal, which
made him less than equal with the Father in substance or
essence, triggered the controversy. He was quickly answered
by Athanasius. In addition to selections from Athanasius's
writings, two brief selections concerning him in Socrates's
*Church History* are also included. The three Cappadocian
Fathers—Basil of Caesarea, Gregory of Nazianzus, and Gregory
of Nyssa—carried the banner of the orthodox view. Selections
from the variety of their writings are included. They were not
only gifted theologians but were also people, and even friends.
Their correspondence reveals their close ties of friendship.
Some readings from Ambrose, bishop of Milan, which reflect

the perspective of the west, are also included. The creeds and related canons from both the Nicene Council (325) and the first Council at Constantinople (381) round out the selections from this crucial period in Christological development.

## EUSEBIUS (C. 264-339)

From the pen of the first church historian, Eusebius's *Church History* chronicles the incubation of the church, telling its story from the time of the apostles to the victory of Constantine at Milvian Bridge (312), which marked the Christianizing of the Roman Empire. His second book, *Life of Constantine*, takes the story from there until the beloved emperor's death. The brief readings from these two works reveal the extent to which the bishops respected Constantine.

*Eusebius, Church History (Historia Ecclesiastica), Book X, Chapter 9;*
*date: 325; source; Nicene and Post-Nicene Fathers, Second Series,*
*Vol. I: Eusebius (Grand Rapids, MI: Eerdmans, 1957), 386-387.*

Thus, suddenly, and sooner than can be told, those who yesterday and the day before breathed death and threatening were no more, and not even their names were remembered, but their inscriptions and their honors suffered the merited disgrace.[1] And the things which Licinius[2] with his own eyes had seen come upon the former impious tyrants he himself likewise suffered, because he did not receive instruction nor learn wisdom from the chastisements of his neighbors, but followed the same path of impiety which they had trod, and was justly hurled over the same precipice. Thus he lay prostrate.

6 But Constantine, the mightiest victor, adorned with every virtue of piety, together with his son Crispus, a most God-beloved prince, and in all respects like his father, recovered the East which belonged to them; and they formed one united Roman empire as of old, bringing under their peaceful sway the whole world from the rising of the sun to the oppo-

site quarter, both north and south, even to the extremities of the declining day.

7 All fear therefore of those who had formerly afflicted them was taken away from men, and they celebrated splendid and festive days. Everything was filled with light, and those who before were downcast beheld each other with smiling faces and beaming eyes. With dances and hymns, in city and country, they glorified first of all God the universal King, because they had been thus taught, and then the pious emperor with his God-beloved children.

8 There was oblivion of past evils and forgetfulness of every deed of impiety; there was enjoyment of present benefits and expectation of those yet to come. Edicts full of clemency and laws containing tokens of benevolence and true piety were issued in every place by the victorious emperor.[3]

9 Thus after all tyranny had been purged away, the empire which belonged to them was preserved firm and without a rival for Constantine and his sons alone. And having obliterated the godlessness of their predecessors, recognizing the benefits conferred upon them by God, they exhibited their love of virtue and their love of God, and their piety and gratitude to the Deity, by the deeds which they performed in the sight of all men.

*Eusebius, Life of Constantine (Vita Constantini), Book I, Chapters 23-24; date: unfinished work, c. 330s; source: Nicene and Post-Nicene Fathers, Second Series, Vol. I, 488-489.*

Chapter 23: With respect to the other princes, who made war against the churches of God, I have not thought it fit in the present work to give any account of their downfall, nor to stain the memory of the good by mentioning them in connection with those of an opposite character. The knowledge of the facts themselves will of itself suffice for the wholesome admonition of those who have witnessed or heard of the evils which severally befell them.

Chapter 24: Thus then the God of all, the Supreme Governor

*what about sovereignty?*

of the whole universe, by his own will appointed Constantine, the descendant of so renowned a parent, to be prince and sovereign: so that, while others have been raised to this distinction by the election of their fellow-men, he is the only one to whose elevation no mortal may boast of having contributed.

## ATHANASIUS (295-373)

The true hero of the story in the fourth century, Athanasius wrote many texts defending the orthodox view and refuting the views of the Arians. Included here are selections from his work *On the Incarnation of the Word* and his shorter pieces, "Defense of the Nicene Creed" and "Defense of Flight." The selection from *On the Incarnation of the Word* lays the groundwork for his Christology by showing humanity's predicament of sin and the need for a Savior who is both fully God and fully human. "Statement of Faith" succinctly reveals his view of Christ. In "Defense of the Nicene Creed," Athanasius stands in as commentator on the proceedings of the Nicene Council. Finally, in "In Defense of Flight," Athanasius chronicles the difficulties for orthodox bishops after the Council of Nicea, who were being persecuted by the Arians. Athanasius himself faced such intense persecution that he had to flee Alexandria; hence the title stems from his defense of fleeing.

*Athanasius, On the Incarnation of the Word (De Incarnatione Verbi), Section 6; date: 335/337; source: Nicene and Post-Nicene Fathers, Second Series, Vol. IV: St. Athanasius (Grand Rapids, MI: Eerdmans, 1957), 39.*

1. For this cause, then, death having gained upon men, and corruption abiding upon them, the race of man was perishing; the rational man made in God's image was disappearing, and the handiwork of God was in process of dissolution. 2. For death, as I said above, gained from that time forth a legal hold over us, and it was impossible to evade the law, since it had been laid down by God because of the transgression, and the

result was in truth at once monstrous and unseemly. 3. For it were monstrous, firstly, that God, having spoken, should prove false—that, when once He had ordained that man, if he transgressed the commandment, should die the death, after the transgression man should not die, but God's word should be broken. For God would not be true, if, when He had said we should die, man died not. 4. Again, it were unseemly that creatures once made rational, and having partaken of the Word, should go to ruin, and turn again toward non-existence by the way of corruption. 5. For it were not worthy of God's goodness that the things He had made should waste away, because of the deceit practiced on men by the devil. 6. Especially it was unseemly to the last degree that God's handicraft among men should be done away, either because of their own carelessness, or because of the deceitfulness of evil spirits.

7. So, as the rational creatures were wasting and such works in course of ruin, what was God in His goodness to do? Suffer corruption to prevail against them and death to hold them fast? And where were the profit of their having been made, to begin with? For better were they not made, than once made, left to neglect and ruin. 8. For neglect reveals weakness, and not goodness on God's part—if, that is, He allows His own work to be ruined when once He had made it—more so than if He had never made man at all. 9. For if He had not made them, none could impute weakness; but once He had made them, and created them out of nothing, it were most monstrous for the work to be ruined, and that before the eyes of the Maker. 10. It was, then, out of the question to leave men to the current of corruption; because this would be unseemly, and unworthy of God's goodness.[4]

     ↳ *No hope w/out Christ*

*Athanasius, "Defense of the Nicene Creed" ("De Decretis Nicaeni Synodi"), Chapter 5; date: 350–351; source: Nicene and Post-Nicene Fathers, Second Series, Vol. IV, 162-163.*

19. The Council wishing to do away with the irreligious phrases of the Arians,[5] and to use instead the acknowledged

words of the Scriptures, that the Son is not from nothing but
"from God," and is "Word" and "Wisdom," and not creature
or work, but a proper offspring from the Father, Eusebius and
his fellows,[6] led by their inveterate heterodoxy, understood the
phrase "from God" as belonging to us, as if in respect to it the
Word of God differed nothing from us, and that because it is
written, "There is one God, from whom, all things"; and again,
"Old things are passed away, behold, all things are become
new, and all things are from God." But the Fathers, perceiving
their craft and the cunning of their irreligion, were forced to
express more distinctly the sense of the words "from God."
Accordingly, they wrote "from the essence of God," in order
that "from God" might not be considered common and equal
in the Son and in things originate, but that all others might be
acknowledged as creatures, and the Word alone as from the
Father. For though all things be said to be from God, yet this
is not in the sense in which the Son is from Him; for as to the
creatures, "of God" is said of them on this account, in that
they exist not at random or spontaneously, nor come to be by
chance, according to those philosophers who refer them to the
combination of atoms, and to elements of similar structure, nor
as certain heretics speak of a distinct Framer, nor as others again
say that the constitution of all things is from certain Angels;
but, in that whereas God is, it was by Him that all things were
brought into being, not being before, through His Word; but as
to the Word, since He is not a creature, He alone is both called
and is "from the Father"; and it is significant of this sense to say
that the Son is "from the essence of the Father," for to nothing
originate does this attach. In truth, when Paul says that "all
things are from God," he immediately adds, "and one Lord
Jesus Christ, through whom all things,"[7] in order to show all
men, that the Son is other than all these things which came to be
from God for the things which came to be from God, came to be
through His Son; and that he had used his foregoing words with
reference to the world as framed by God, and not as if all things

were from the Father as the Son is. For neither are other things as the Son, nor is the Word one among others, for He is Lord and Framer of all; and on this account did the Holy Council declare expressly that He was of the essence of the Father,[8] that we might believe the Word to be other than the nature of things originate, being alone truly from God; and that no subterfuge should be left open to the irreligious. This then was the reason why the Council wrote "of the essence."

*homoousion*

*Athanasius, "Defense of Flight" ("Apoligia de Fuga Sua"); date: 356; source: Nicene and Post-Nicene Fathers, Second Series, Vol. IV, 256.*

For whom have they ever persecuted and taken, that they have not insulted and injured as they pleased? Whom have they ever sought after and found, that they have not handled in such a manner, that either he has died a miserable death, or has been ill-treated in every way? Whatever the magistrates appear to do, it is their work; and the others are merely the tools of their will and wickedness.[9] In consequence, where is there a place that has not some memorial of their malice? Who has ever opposed them, without their conspiring against him, inventing pretexts for his ruin after the manner of Jezebel? Where is there a Church that is not at this moment lamenting the success of their plots against her Bishops? Antioch is mourning for the orthodox Confessor Eustathius; Laneae for the most admirable Euphration, Paltus and Antaradus for Kymatius and Carterius; Adrianople for that lover of Christ, Eutropius, and his successor Lucius, who was often loaded with chains by their means, and so perished; Ancyra mourns for Marcellus, Berthoea for Cyrus, Gaza for Asclepas. Of all these, after inflicting many outrages, they by their intrigues procured the banishment; but for Theodulus and Olympius, Bishops of Thrace, and for us and our Presbyters, they caused diligent search to be made, to the intent that if we were discovered we should suffer capital punishment: and probably we should have so perished, had we not fled at that very time contrary to their intentions.[10] For letters to that effect were delivered to the

Proconsul Donatus against Olympius and his fellows, and to Philagrius against me. And having raised a persecution against Paul, Bishop of Constantinople, as soon as they found him, they caused him to be openly strangled at a place called Cucusus in Cappadocia, employing as their executioner for the purpose Philip, who was Prefect. He was a patron of their heresy, and the tool of their wicked designs.

## SOCRATES (C. 381-C. 440S)

Born at Constantinople, Socrates lived during the fifth century and authored a history of the church that spans from 306 until 439. The first brief selection from his *Church History* tells of Athanasius's clever eluding of authorities on one occasion (Book III, Chapter 14). The second provides an account of his death (Book IV, Chapter 20).

*Socrates, Church History (Historiae Ecclesiasticae), Book III, Chapter 14;*
*date: c. 440; source: Nicene and Post-Nicene Fathers, Second Series, Vol. II:*
*Socrates and Sozemenus (Grand Rapids, MI: Eerdmans, 1957), 86.*

But he [Athanasius] fled again, saying to his intimates, "Let us retire for a little while, friends; it is but a small cloud which will soon pass away." He then immediately embarked, and crossing the Nile, hastened with all speed into Egypt, closely pursued by those who sought to take him. When he understood that his pursuers were not far distant, his attendants were urging him to retreat once more into the desert, but he had recourse to an artifice and thus effected his escape.[11] He persuaded those who accompanied him to turn back and meet his adversaries, which they did immediately; and on approaching them they were simply asked "where they had seen Athanasius?" To which they replied that "he was not a great way off," and, that "if they hastened they would soon overtake him." Being thus deluded, they started afresh in pursuit with quickened speed, but to no purpose; and Athanasius making good his retreat, returned secretly to

Alexandria; and there he remained concealed until the persecution was at an end. Such were the perils which succeeded one another in the career of the bishop of Alexandria, these last from the heathen coming after that to which he was before subjected from Christians. In addition to these things, the governors of the provinces taking advantage of the emperor's superstition to feed their own cupidity, committed more grievous outrages on the Christians than their sovereign had given them a warrant for; sometimes exacting larger sums of money than they ought to have done, and at others inflicting on them corporal punishments. The emperor[12] learning of these excesses, connived at them; and when the sufferers appealed to him against their oppressors, he tauntingly said, "It is your duty to bear these afflictions patiently; for this is the command of your God."

*Socrates, Church History, Book IV, Chapter 20, 105.*

It must be said that as long as Athanasius, bishop of Alexandria, was alive, the emperor, restrained by the Providence of God, abstained from molesting Alexandria and Egypt: indeed he knew very well that the multitude of those who were attached to Athanasius was very great; and on that account he was careful lest the public affairs should be hazarded, by the Alexandrians, who are an irritable race, being excited to sedition. But Athanasius, after being engaged in so many and such severe conflicts on behalf of the church, departed this life in the second consulate of Gratian and Probus, having governed that church amidst the greatest perils forty-six years.

## BASIL OF CAESAREA (C. 329-379)

The first of the three Cappadocian Fathers, Basil was brother to Gregory of Nyssa and a close friend from university days with Gregory of Nazianzus. He presided over the Council of Constantinople (381). Among his writings is his *On the Holy Spirit*, a robust defense of Trinitarianism in light of the Arian controversy. The first selection here comes from the beginning and shows how crucial subtleties were to the whole debate, as well as how grueling the debate became. But, he argues, the issue demands his involvement. In the next reading, from later in the work—Chapter 30—he gives us further insight into the "tempest" set off by the Arian controversy in the church. These were troubling times.

*Basil, On The Holy Spirit (De Spiritu Sancto), Chapter 1; date: c. 370; source: Nicene and Post-Nicene Fathers, Second Series, Vol. VIII: Basil (Grand Rapids, MI: Eerdmans, 1957), 2-3.*

If any one laughs when he sees our subtlety, to use the Psalmist's words, about syllables,[3] let him know that he reaps laughter's fruitless fruit; and let us, neither giving in to men's reproaches, nor yet vanquished by their disparagement, continue our investigation. So far, indeed, am I from feeling ashamed of these things because they are small, that, even if I could attain to ever so minute a fraction of their dignity, I should both congratulate myself on having won high honor, and should tell my brother and fellow-investigator that no small gain had accrued to him there from.

While, then, I am aware that the controversy contained in little words is a very great one, in hope of the prize I do not shrink from toil, with the conviction that the discussion will both prove profitable to myself, and that my hearers will be rewarded with no small benefit.

*Basil, On the Holy Spirit, Chapter 30, 48.*

To what then shall I liken our present condition?[14] It may be compared, I think, to some naval battle which has arisen out of time old quarrels, and is fought by men who cherish a deadly hate against one another, of long experience in naval warfare, and eager for the fight. Look, I beg you, at the picture thus raised before your eyes. See the rival fleets rushing in dread array to the attack. With a burst of uncontrollable fury they engage and fight it out. Fancy, if you like, the ships driven to and fro by a raging tempest, while thick darkness falls from the clouds and blackens all the scenes so that watchwords are indistinguishable in the confusion, and all distinction between friend and foe is lost. To fill up the details of the imaginary picture, suppose the sea swollen with billows and whirled up from the deep, while a vehement torrent of rain pours down from the clouds and the terrible waves rise high. From every quarter of heaven the winds beat upon one point, where both the fleets are dashed one against the other. Of the combatants some are turning traitors; some are deserting in the very thick of the fight; some have at one and the same moment to urge on their boats, all beaten by the gale, and to advance against their assailants. Jealousy of authority and the lust of individual mastery splits the sailors into parties which deal mutual death to one another. Think, besides all this, of the confused and unmeaning roar sounding over all the sea, from howling winds, from crashing vessels, from boiling surf, from the yells of the combatants as they express their varying emotions in every kind of noise, so that not a word from admiral or pilot can be heard. The disorder and confusion is tremendous, for the extremity of misfortune, when life is despaired of, gives men license for every kind of wickedness. Suppose, too, that the men are all smitten with the incurable plague of mad love of glory, so that they do not cease from their struggle each to get the better of the other, while their ship is actually settling down into the deep.

## GREGORY OF NAZIANZUS (329-390)

Basil's close friend from their days at the University of Athens, Gregory of Nazianzus too arose, rather reluctantly, to the office of bishop. His writings also catapulted him to the center of the controversy. From his many "Orations" comes "Oration 33," commonly called "Against the Arians." At the end of the oration he sets forth his own beliefs on the person of Christ. In addition to his "Orations," Gregory of Nazianzus is known for his many epistles. In fact, he wrote guidelines for letter writing, extolling brevity, clarity, and eloquence. One letter to Basil and one to Gregory of Nyssa are included here, revealing the close ties of these three and their mutual encouragement in light of the challenge of battling heretics. A final selection is Gregory's memorial poem on his friendship with Basil.

*Gregory of Nazianzus, Oration 33, "Against the Arians," Paragraph 17; date: 380; source: Nicene and Post-Nicene Fathers, Second Series, Vol. VII: Cyril of Jerusalem, Gregory of Nazianzen (Grand Rapids, MI: Eerdmans, 1957), 334.*

These words let everyone who threatens me today concede to me; the rest let whoever will claim. The Father will not endure to be deprived of the Son, nor the Son of the Holy Ghost. Yet that must happen if They are confined to time, and are created Beings . . . for that which is created is not God. Neither will I bear to be deprived of my consecration; One Lord, One Faith, One Baptism. If this be cancelled, from whom shall I get a second? What say you, you who destroy Baptism or repeat it? Can a man be spiritual without the Spirit? Has he a share in the Spirit who does not honor the Spirit? Can he honor Him who is baptized into a creature and a fellow-servant? It is not so; it is not so; for all your talk. I will not play Thee false, O Unoriginate Father, or Thee O Only-begotten Word, or Thee O Holy Ghost. I know Whom I have confessed, and Whom I have renounced, and to Whom I have joined myself. I will not allow myself, after having been taught the words of the faithful, to learn also those of the unfaithful; to confess the truth, and then range myself with falsehood; to come down for consecration and to go back even less hallowed; having been baptized that I might live, to be killed by the water, like infants who die in the very birth pangs, and receive death simultaneously with birth.[15] Why make me at once blessed and wretched, newly enlightened and unenlightened, Divine and godless, that I may make shipwreck even of the hope of regeneration? A few words will suffice. Remember your confession. Into what were you baptized? The Father? Good but Jewish still. The Son? . . . good . . . but not yet perfect. The Holy Ghost? . . . Very good . . . this is perfect. Now was it into these simply, or some common name of Them? The latter. And what was the common Name? Why, God.[16] In this common Name believe, and ride on prosperously and reign, and pass on from hence into the Bliss of Heaven. And that is, as I think, the more distinct apprehension of These; to which may we all come, in the same Christ our God, to Whom be the glory and the might, with the Unoriginate Father, and the Lifegiving Spirit, now and for ever and to ages of ages. Amen.

*Gregory of Nazianzus, Letters, #8, to Basil; date: 362; source: Nicene and Post-Nicene Fathers, Second Series, Vol. VII, 448.*

I approve the beginning of your letter; but what is there of yours that I do not approve? And you are convicted of having written just like me; for I, too, was forced into the rank of the Priesthood, for indeed I never was eager for it. We are to one another, if ever any men were, trustworthy witnesses of our love for a humble and lowly philosophy. But perhaps it would have been better that this had not happened, or I know not what to say, as long as I am in ignorance of the purpose of the Holy Ghost. But since it has come about, we must bear it, at least so it seems clear to me; and especially when we take the times into consideration, which are bringing in upon us so many heretical tongues, and must not put to shame either the hopes of those who have trusted us thus, or our own lives.

*Gregory of Nazianzus, Letters, #72, to Gregory of Nyssa; date: 378; source: Nicene and Post-Nicene Fathers, Second Series, Vol. VII, 460.*

Do not let your troubles distress you too much. For the less we grieve over things, the less grievous they are. It is nothing strange that the heretics have thawed, and are taking courage from the springtime, and creeping out of their holes, as you write. They will hiss for a short time, I know, and then will hide themselves again, overcome both by the truth and the times, and all the more so the more we commit the whole matter to God.

*Gregory of Nazianzus, poem on his friendship with Basil; date: ?; source: Nicene and Post-Nicene Fathers, Second Series, Vol. VII, 190.*

> *For God had given me yet one priceless gift*
> *Uniting me with Wisdom's wisest son,*
> *Himself alone above all life and word;*
> *Who this could be you soon shall know full well;*
> *Basil his name; our age's great support.*
> *He was the comrade of my words and roof,*
> *And of my thoughts, if I may boast so much,*
> *A pair were we not all unknown in Greece;[17]*
> *All things we shared in common, and one soul*
> *Linked us together, though in body twain.*
> *One thing there was which joined us most of all,*
> *The love of God and of the highest good.*
> *For, soon as courage came to us to speak*
> *Each to the other of that we had at heart,*
> *More closely were our spirits knit in love,*
> *For fellow feeling makes us wondrous kind.*

## GREGORY OF NYSSA (335-395)

The third of the Cappadocian Fathers, Gregory was brother to Basil. He wrote a lengthy refutation of one of the main proponents of Arianism, Eunomius, bishop of Cyzicus from 360–364. After Eunomius was deposed as bishop, he became the leader of the extreme Arian group referred to as the Anomoeans. This group is named for the Greek word *anomoios*, meaning "unlike," which refers to their view that Christ is unlike the Father. To further confuse things, sometimes these folks are called Eunomians, after their founder's name. The view of Eunomius that Jesus is unlike the Father even goes beyond the view of Arius, who held that the Son is of a similar substance (*homoiousion*) with the Father. In the first selection from *Against Eunomius*, Book I, section 18, Gregory boils the whole controversy down to one question: Were Christ and the Holy Spirit made or not? The next selection colorfully states what Gregory thinks of Eunomius's view.

The next two selections come from shorter pieces. From "On Not Three Gods," Gregory offers a short but compelling explanation of the oneness of the three persons of the Trinity. In "On the Faith," he gives a thorough statement of his belief in Christ as fully God and fully human.

*Gregory of Nyssa (Against Eunomius) (Contra Eunomium), Book 1, Section 18; date: c. 380–383; source: Nicene and Post-Nicene Fathers, Second Series, Vol. V: Gregory of Nyssa (Grand Rapids, MI: Eerdmans, 1957), 56.*

The whole controversy, then, between the Church and the Anomoeans[18] turns on this: Are we to regard the Son and the Holy Spirit as belonging to created or uncreated existence? Our opponent declares that to be the case which all deny: he boldly lays it down, without looking about for any proof, that each being is the work of the preceding being. What method of education, what school of thought can warrant him in this, it is difficult to see. Some axiom that cannot be denied or assailed must be the beginning of every process of proof; so as for the unknown quantity to be demonstrated from what has been assumed, being legitimately deduced by intervening syllogisms. The reasoner, therefore, who makes what ought to be the object of inquiry itself a premise of his demonstration is only proving the obscure by the obscure, and illusion by illusion. He is making "the blind lead the blind," for it is a truly blind and unsupported statement to say that the Creator and Maker of all things is a creature made: and to this they link on a conclusion that is also blind: namely, that the Son is alien in nature, *unlike* in being to the Father, and quite devoid of His essential character. But enough of this. Where his thought is nakedly blasphemous, there we too can defer its refutation. We must now return to consider his words which come next in order.

*Gregory of Nyssa, Against Eunomius, Book 10, Section 4; source: Nicene and Post-Nicene Fathers, Second Series, Vol. V, 228.*

Let us however return once more to the course of his treatise. What does Eunomius say concerning the Only-begotten? That He "does not appropriate the dignity," for he calls the appellation of "being" a "dignity." A startling piece of philosophy! Who of all men that have ever been, whether among Greeks or barbarian sages, who of the men of our own day, who of the men of all time ever gave "being" the name of "dignity"? For everything that is regarded as subsisting is said, by the common custom of all who use language, to "be": and from the word "be" has been formed the term "being." But now the expression "dignity" is applied in a new fashion to the idea expressed by "being." For he says that "the Son, Who is and lives because of the Father, does not appropriate this dignity," having no Scripture to support his statement, and not conducting his statement to so senseless a conclusion by any process of logical inference, but as if he had taken into his intestines some windy food, he belches forth his blasphemy in its crude and unmethodized form, like some unsavory breath. "He does not appropriate this dignity." Let us concede the point of "being" being called "dignity." What then? Does He Who is not appropriate being? "No," says Eunomius, "because He exists by reason of the Father." Do you not then say that He Who does not appropriate being is not? For "not to appropriate" has the same force as "to be alien from," and the mutual opposition of the ideas is evident. For that which is "proper" is not "alien," and that which is "alien" is not "proper." He therefore Who does not "appropriate" being is obviously alien from being: and He Who is alien from being is nonexistent.

*Gregory of Nyssa, "On Not Three Gods" ("Quod Non Sint Tres Dei"); date: ?; source: Nicene and Post-Nicene Fathers, Second Series, Vol. V, 336.*

But the word "God" [Scripture] employs studiously in the singular form only, guarding against introducing the idea of different natures in the Divine essence by the plural signification of "Gods." This is the cause why it says, "the Lord our God is one Lord," and also proclaims the Only-begotten God by the name of Godhead, without dividing the Unity into a dual signification, so as to call the Father and the Son two Gods, although each is proclaimed by the holy writers as God. The Father is God: the Son is God: and yet by the same proclamation God is One, because no difference either of nature or of operation is contemplated in the Godhead. For if, according to the idea of those who have been led astray, the nature of the Holy Trinity were diverse, the number would by consequence be extended to a plurality of Gods, being divided according to the diversity of essence in the subjects. But since the Divine, single, and unchanging nature, that it may be one, rejects all diversity in essence, it does not admit in its own case the signification of multitude.

*Gregory of Nyssa, "On the Faith" ("De Professione"); date: ?; source: Nicene and Post-Nicene Fathers, Second Series, Vol. V, 338.*

For the Apostle says that the Son is the express image of the Person of the Father.[19] It is clear then that however great the Person of the Father is, so great also is the express image of that Person; for it is not possible that the express image should be less than the Person contemplated in it. And this the great John also teaches when he says, "In the beginning was the Word, and the Word was with God." For in saying that he was "in the beginning" and not "after the beginning," he showed that the beginning was never without the Word; and in declaring that "the Word was with God," he signified the absence of defect in the Son in relation to the Father; for the Word is contemplated as a whole together with the whole being of God. For if the Word were deficient in His own greatness so as not to be capable of relation with the whole being of God, we are compelled to suppose that that part of God which extends beyond the Word is without the Word. But in fact the whole magnitude of the Word is contemplated together with the whole magnitude of God: and consequently in statements concerning the Divine nature, it is not admissible to speak of "greater" and "less."[20]

## AMBROSE (C. 339-397)

Adding a western voice to the bishops of the east, these selections from Ambrose, bishop at Milan, reveal how committed he was to the Nicene Creed and against the Arians. His *Of the Christian Faith* was occasioned by a request from the emperor in the West, Gratian (375–383). In the prologue Ambrose stresses the priority of matters of faith, and he offers his high estimation of the Nicene Creed. In Chapter 1 he sets forth the orthodox view, while in Chapter 5 he succinctly runs down Arian beliefs.

*Ambrose, Of the Christian Faith (De Fide), Book 1, Chapter 1; date: 378; source: Nicene and Post-Nicene Fathers, Second Series, Vol. X: St. Ambrose (Grand Rapids, MI: Eerdmans, 1957), 202-203.*

6. Now this is the declaration of our Faith, that we say that God is One, neither dividing His Son from Him, as do the heathen, nor denying, with the Jews, that He was begotten of the Father before all worlds, and afterwards born of the Virgin; nor yet, like Sabellius, confounding the Father with the Word, and so maintaining that Father and Son are one and the same Person; nor again, as doth Photinus, holding that the Son first came into existence in the Virgin's womb: nor believing, with Arius, in a number of diverse Powers, and so, like the benighted heathen, making out more than one God. For it is written: "Hear, O Israel: the Lord thy God is one God."

9. Moreover, Christ Himself says: "I and the Father are One." "One," said He, that there be no separation of power and nature; but again, "*We are,*" that you may recognize Father and Son, forasmuch as the perfect Father is believed to have begotten the perfect Son, and the Father and the Son are One, not by confusion of Person, but by unity of nature.

10. We say, then, that there is one God, not two or three Gods, this being the error into which the impious heresy of the Arians doth run with its blasphemies. For it says that there are three Gods, in that it divides the Godhead of the Trinity; whereas the Lord, in saying, "Go, baptize the nations in the name of the Father and of the Son and of the Holy Spirit," hath shown that the Trinity is of one power. We confess Father, Son, and Spirit, understanding in a perfect Trinity both fullness of Divinity and unity of power.

11. "Every kingdom divided against itself shall quickly be overthrown," says the Lord. Now the kingdom of the Trinity is not divided. If, therefore, it is not divided, it is one; for that which is not one is divided. The Arians, however, would have the kingdom of the Trinity to be such as may easily be overthrown, by division against itself. But truly, seeing that it cannot be overthrown, it is plainly undivided. For no unity is divided or rent asunder, and therefore neither age nor corruption has any power over it.

*Ambrose, Of the Christian Faith, Book 1, Chapter 5; source: Nicene and Post-Nicene Fathers, Second Series, Vol. X, 206-207.*

34. Now let us consider the disputings of the Arians concerning the Son of God.

35. They say that the Son of God is unlike His Father. To say this of a man would be an insult.

36. They say that the Son of God had a beginning in time, whereas He Himself is the source and ordainer of time and all that therein is. We are men, and we would not be limited to time. We began to exist once, and we believe that we shall have

a timeless existence. We desire after immortality—how, then, can we deny the eternity of God's Son, Whom God declares to be eternal by nature, not by grace?

37. They say that He was created. But who would reckon an author with his works, and have him seem to be what he has himself made?

38. They deny His goodness. Their blaspheming is its own condemnation, and so cannot hope for pardon.

39. They deny that He is truly Son of God, they deny His omnipotence, in that while they admit that all things are made by the ministry of the Son, they attribute the original source of their being to the power of God. But what is power, save perfection of nature?

40. Furthermore, the Arians deny that in Godhead He is One with the Father. Let them annul the Gospel, then, and silence the voice of Christ. For Christ Himself has said: "I and the Father are one." It is not I who say this: Christ has said it. Is He a deceiver, that He should lie? Is He unrighteous, that He should claim to be what He never was? But of these matters we will deal severally, at greater length, in their proper place.

41. Seeing, then, that the heretic says that Christ is unlike His Father, and seeks to maintain this by force of subtle disputation, we must cite the Scripture: "Take heed that no man make spoil of you by philosophy and vain deceit, according to the tradition of men, and after the rudiments of this world, not according to Christ; for in Him dwells all the fullness of Godhead in bodily shape."

42. For they store up all the strength of their poisons in dialectical disputation, which by the judgment of philosophers is defined as having no power to establish aught, and aiming only at destruction. But it was not by dialectic that it pleased God to save His people; "for the kingdom of God consists in simplicity of faith, not in wordy contention."

## ARIUS (C. 250-336)

It was Arius, presbyter at Alexandria, who set off the great controversy in the 300s. In this letter he protests his condemnation, claiming that all he has taught is that Christ is not eternal.

*Arius, Letter to Eusebius of Nicomedia; date: c. 319.*

To his very dear lord, the man of God, the faithful and orthodox Eusebius, Arius, unjustly persecuted by Alexander the Pope, on account of that all conquering truth of which you also are a champion, sends greeting in the Lord.

Ammonius, my father, being about to depart for Nicomedia, I considered myself bound to salute you by him, and withal to inform that natural affection which you bear towards the brethren for the sake of God and His Christ, that the bishop greatly wastes and persecutes us, and leaves no stone unturned against us. He has driven us out of the city as atheists, because we do not concur in what he publicly preaches, namely, God always, the Son always; as the Father so the Son; the Son co-exists unbegotten with the God; He is everlasting; neither by thought nor by any interval does God precede the Son; always God, always Son; he is begotten of the unbegotten; the Son is of God Himself. . . .

We are persecuted, because we say that the Son has a beginning,[21] but that God is without beginning. This is the cause of our persecution, and likewise, because we say that He is of the non-existent. And this we say, because He is neither part of God, nor of any essential being. For this are we persecuted; the rest you know. I bid thee farewell in the Lord, remembering our afflictions, my fellow-Lucianist, and true Eusebius.

## THE FORMS OF THE NICENE-CONSTANTINOPOLITAN CREED

The Creed agreed upon at 325 needed to be reaffirmed after decades of Arian dominance in the church. Consequently, the

Council at Constantinople in 381 largely made definitive what had already been hashed out and stated earlier in 325 at the Nicene Council. The Nicene Creed includes an "anathema" paragraph, condemning those who would reject the first paragraph. Constantinople moves the anathema section from the Creed to its position as the first canon. Canon I also lists specific heresies that are condemned.

*The Creed from the Council at Nicea; date: 325.*

We believe in one God, the Father Almighty, maker of all things visible and invisible, and in one Lord Jesus Christ, the son of God, the only begotten of his Father, of the substance of the Father, God of God, Light of Light, very God of very God, begotten, not made, being of one substance with [*homoousion*] the Father.[22] By whom all things were made, both which are in heaven and in earth. Who for us and for our salvation came down from heaven and was incarnate and was made man. He suffered and the third day he rose again, and ascended into heaven. And he shall come again to judge both the quick and the dead. And we believe in the Holy Ghost.

And whosoever shall say that there was a time when the Son of God was not, or that before he was begotten he was not, or that he is of a different substance or essence from the Father, or that he is a creature, or subject to change or conversion—all that so say, the Catholic and Apostolic Church anathematizes them.[23]

*The Creed from the Council at Constantinople, commonly recited today as the "Nicene Creed"; date: 381.*

We believe in one God, the Father Almighty, maker of heaven and earth, and of all things visible and invisible. And in one Lord Jesus Christ, the only begotten Son of God, begotten of his Father before all worlds, Light of Light, very God of very God, begotten not made, being of one substance with [*homoou-*

*sion*] the Father, by whom all things were made. Who for us and
for our salvation came down from heaven and was incarnate by
the Holy Ghost and the Virgin Mary, and was made man, and
was crucified also for us under Pontius Pilate. He suffered and
(was buried,) and the third day he rose again (according to the
scriptures,) and ascended into heaven, and sitteth at the right
hand of the Father. And he shall come again with glory to judge
the quick and the dead. (Whose kingdom shall have no end.)

And we believe in the Holy Ghost, the Lord and Giver of
life, who proceeds from the Father,[24] who with the Father and
the Son is worshipped and glorified, who spoke by the prophets.
And we believe in one, holy, catholic, and apostolic church. We
acknowledge one baptism for the forgiveness of sins, and we
look for the resurrection of the dead and the life of the world
to come.

*Canon I of the Council of Constantinople; date: 381.*

The Faith of the Three Hundred and Eighteen Fathers
assembled at Nicea in Bythinia shall not be set aside but shall
remain firm. And every heresy shall be anathematized, particularly that of the Eunomians (or the Anomoeans), the Arians (or
Eudoxians), and that of the Semi-Arians or Pneumatomochi,
and that of the Sabellians, and that of the Marcellians, and that
of the Photinians, and that of the Apollinarians.

## CHAPTER FIVE

# The Wisdom of Leo the Great:
# The Battle for Christ at Chalcedon

*For it must again and again be repeated that one and the same
is truly Son of God and truly son of man.*

LEO'S "TOME"

**W**hen Johann Sebastian Bach composed the music for the section on the Creed in his *Mass in B Minor*, he revealed his skill not just at music, but also at theology. He used full voice choirs in his musical telling of the Nicene Creed, except in two pieces. In one, "*Et in Spiritum Sanctum*," treating the final clauses of the Creed, which relate to the Holy Spirit, he employed an aria with a solo bass voice. In another, "*Et in unum Dominum*," treating the Creed's central points about Christ, he has a duet, with soprano and alto voices gracefully extolling belief in the deity and the humanity of Christ. Bach has each voice sing the Christ-centered phrases of the Creed in succession before weaving them together in one unified chorus. Bach was musically doing for the Nicene Creed what the Chalcedonian Creed would do for it theologically: bring the two natures of Christ, his full humanity and his full deity, into one undivided, unconfused, and unmixed person. Chalcedon and Bach tell us there are two distinct and individual natures forming one unified person, two voices forming one grand choir.[1]

Bach's *Mass in B Minor* is a musical accomplishment to be sure, perhaps the finest in all of church music (next to

Luther's "A Mighty Fortress Is Our God"—but I'm biased). Equally excellent is the level of theological accomplishment at Chalcedon. Chalcedon threaded the Gordian knot of expressing the union of the human and divine natures, natures that are diametrically opposed, in a way that avoided diminishing either nature, all the while being true to Scripture. What's more, Chalcedon is nothing short of miraculous considering that its creed and canons, dealing with very sophisticated and complex issues, are the result of the unanimous consent of 520 bishops. Try getting 520 contemporary church leaders to agree on anything, much less the intricate issues that Chalcedon treats, and you'll see why it borders on the miraculous. While the creed benefited from the combined efforts of these bishops, the crucial

## HOW DID THE BISHOP IN ROME BECOME POPE?

By the end of the first century, the office of the bishop rose to prominence in the early church. The letters of Ignatius reveal the bishop guiding the church in the face of controversy and heresy. In the second century, bishops like Polycarp and Irenaeus furthered this trajectory of the bishops' leadership of the church. In these first five centuries, however, the leadership mostly resided in the plurality of the bishops. At times one bishop would rise to prominence, and at times rivalries would heat up between bishoprics. The divided empire gave further rise to rivalry between Rome and Constantinople. Leo the Great, for instance, refused to submit to Constantinople. Eventually these two churches would split, forming the Orthodox Church in the east and the Roman Catholic Church in the west. Given a series of competent and capable bishops at Rome, that city and its bishop rose to prominence in the western church. The move from bishop of Rome to papacy took a giant step forward in 444 when Leo, as bishop of Rome, was made the head of the church in the west. Gregory the Great, whom the world knows today through his legacy of the Gregorian chant, completed the move. He asserted that the bishop of Rome had always been the de facto leader of the church and was the true successor to the apostle Peter. Gregory's use of history was rather selective at best. Roman Catholics trace a line of succession from Peter to the present day, whereas Protestants tend to see the papacy beginning with Gregory the Great in 590.

phrase, the phrase that mattered, resulted from the work of one bishop—Leo of Rome, sometimes called Leo the Great. In a letter just prior to the council, which Leo himself actually did not attend, he expressed what most today take for granted as the orthodox definition of Christ as *two natures in one person.* This chapter tells his story.[2]

## FACING DOWN ATTILA THE HUN

Leo was no stranger to controversy, and he had plenty of experience in difficult negotiations. The fifth-century Byzantine historian Priscus relates the tale of Leo the Great's encounter with Attila the Hun. Busy sacking Europe, Attila had long set his sights on Rome. Valentinian III, emperor in the west from 425–455, corresponded often with Leo on "the Attila problem." In the end it was agreed that Leo would seek a private audience with the conqueror to appeal to the better angels of his nature. Attila agreed, and the two met privately on the banks of the Mincius River, where Attila's army camped dangerously close. No one knows exactly what passed between the leader of the church and the leader of the Huns. But whatever was said, it had an enormous impact on history. Attila backed his army away, headed over the Alps, and returned home beyond the Danube. Rome was safe for the time being.[3]

Later church officials declared the conversation on the banks of the Mincius a miracle, gaining sainthood for Leo in the Roman Catholic Church. Historians think that the Huns' distinct lack of supplies for the army and a severe famine in the region had something to do with it as well. Not to be missed, however, is the conversation. Attila, a pagan king, would not be automatically inclined to placate Leo, a Christian bishop. Leo knew the timely word for the occasion. On top of wisdom, he also evinced courage. Both traits served him well in the theological battles he faced.

These theological battles were long in the making. Arianism

was waning by the 370s and would be condemned, for the second time, at the Council of Constantinople in 381. Arianism wasn't, however, the only challenge facing the early church in its development of the doctrine of Christ. In the late 300s the teachings of Apollinarius (315–392), bishop of Laodicea from 361 until he was condemned in 377, rocked the ever-troubled waters. Later edicts by the Emperor Theodosius in the early 380s would further ostracize the former bishop. Nevertheless, Apollinarius continued to write and teach until his death in 392. His followers, known as Apollinarians, would also flourish for the next decades until meeting a decisive blow at the Council of Chalcedon in 451.

Apollinarius started off his theological endeavors by attempting to put down Arianism and to defend Athanasius and the Nicene Creed. He and his father were well acquainted with Athanasius, hosting him in their home on Athanasius's return from one of his exiles. Apollinarius, however, went too far in his defense of Athanasius. In his zeal he ended up swinging the pendulum way to the right. In overemphasizing the deity of Christ, contrary to Arianism, Apollinarius compromised the humanity of Christ. Starting with good intentions, Apollinarius ended his theological endeavors outside the bounds of orthodoxy.

In order to understand his position we have to understand Apollinarius's view of human nature. Apollinarius, influenced by the teaching of Plato, understood human nature to be composed of three parts: body, a sensitive soul, and a rational soul. Further, he held that the will resided in the rational soul. In order to preserve Christ's deity, Apollinarius was unwilling to grant that Christ had a human will, which for him could be nothing but sinful, and therefore Christ did not have a human rational soul. In fact, the soul of Christ was divine, what Apollinarius saw in the Bible as the *Logos*. The Divine *Logos*, Christ's divine nature, replaced the human rational soul in the person of Christ. The upshot of all this is that Apollinarius viewed Christ as the

God-man in the following way: he was human in possessing a
human body and a human sensitive soul, and he was divine in
possessing the divine rational soul or *Logos*. To put the problem
with his thinking directly, Apollinarius denied the full humanity
of Jesus Christ.

Further, Apollinarius's view of the union of the divine and
human natures laid the groundwork for yet another controversy, which would come to be called *monophysitism*. Not a
word you hear every day, this needs some unpacking. *Physos*
is the Greek word for "nature" (*naturam* in Latin, a word
that was then transliterated into English). *Mono* means "one."
Taken together, this word literally means that Christ is one
nature. Fleshing out this bare-bones definition, Christ is not
two natures, human and divine, in one person, but simply one
nature/person, a God-man without a clearly defined and distinct humanity and deity. We'll revisit monophysitism shortly
in discussing the controversy around Eutyches. It is enough to
say for now that Apollinarianism, in an attempt to preserve
the deity of Christ in light of the Arian threat, created a whole
new set of problems. It overcorrected the problem, spawning a
whole new one.

The church wrestled with Apollinarianism throughout
the 360s and 370s, sending Basil and Gregory of Nyssa, two
of the three Cappadocian Fathers mentioned in Chapter 3,
to do its bidding. Basil corresponded often with Apollinarius
and esteemed him highly for both his skill at theology and his
piety. Jerome, one of the most significant of the church fathers
and one of Apollinarius's students, also spoke glowingly of
Apollinarius. Because of Apollinarius's skill, as well as the
depths of his devotion, his teachings found a stronghold in his
followers. Despite their condemnations they managed to hold
on, eking out a splinter group in the early church. The decisive
blow would come at Chalcedon.

## POLITICS AND THEOLOGY

This theological controversy raged on between the two schools of thought, the Antiochene school and the Alexandrian school. These two schools, taking their names from the cities where these two different teachings flourished, represented two distinct approaches to understanding Christ as the God-man. In reality these two schools represented two different approaches to theology in general. The issues revolving around Christ, like the proverbial tip of the iceberg, simply became the flashpoint. Nestorius came to be the chief proponent of the Antiochene school. Nestorius (381–451), bishop at Constantinople, met his match in Cyril, bishop at Alexandria. What on the surface, and in many of the history books, looks to be a theological controversy may also have a lot to do with politics—church politics, that is.[4]

### CONTROVERSIES AT CHALCEDON

| Apollinarianism | Apollinarius of Laodicea (315–392) | Denies full humanity of Christ; Divine *Logos* replaces human spirit |
| --- | --- | --- |
| Nestorianism | Nestorius of Constantinople (381–451) | Denies unity of person by stress on two natures |
| Eutychianism | Eutyches of Constantinople (c. 378–454) | Christ is neither divine nor human, but a new, singular nature; denies the two, distinct natures of Christ |

As for theology, the Antiochene school tended to view Christ's two natures, the human and divine, along the lines of what they termed the word/human, or *Logos/anthropos* (both words being English transliterations of Greek words). The Alexandrians tended to refer to the distinction as word/flesh, or *Logos/sarx* (*sarx* is the Greek word for "flesh"). The word/flesh view was developed first by Athanasius and later by Cyril of Alexandria, who was bishop from 412 to 444. They both took their cue from the Gospel of John's prologue: "The Word [*Logos*] became flesh [*sarx*]." They viewed the flesh as corruptible. Christ, the *Logos*, the divine being, took on flesh, *sarx*, the full human condition of corruption. And in doing so, Christ as the God-man in the incarnation and in the atonement transforms and redeems corruptible humanity. Christ is fully human—body, soul, and spirit—and fully divine, but he is also the Word made flesh as one unified, singular person. Nestorius drifted from this teaching by substituting the word "human" as his understanding of the word "flesh." In Nestorius's hands, the Antiochene school took a dangerous turn away from Athanasius and Cyril.[5]

Cyril and the Alexandrian theologians took issue with the Nestorian version of Antiochene theology, especially Nestorius's language of the word/human. As Cyril listened to Nestorius, he heard him saying that Christ is two persons, two "he's." What Cyril wanted to hear was that Jesus was one "he," one person. Nestorius so stressed the humanity and divinity of Christ that he veered very near to saying that the two natures are so distinct in Christ that Christ is a divided person, a human person and divine person, that Christ is two "he's" and not merely two natures. Nestorius would even point to specific instances in the Gospels where the human Jesus was present and to other places where the divine Jesus was present. For Nestorius, it's not Jesus Christ *is*. Instead, it's Jesus Christ *are*, which is both grammatically and theologically incorrect.

Bitter rivalry dogged these theologians, and the dialogue between the two suffered. After councils at Ephesus (431) and Chalcedon (451) condemned Nestorius, he would not only affirm that Christ is two natures and one person but would insist that he held to this view all along and was only misunderstood. His own protestations notwithstanding, Nestorius is likely guilty of overplaying the two natures and underplaying the unity of Christ in his one person. There may have been politics involved, but Nestorius rightly deserved Cyril's and Chalcedon's condemnation.

## YELLOW AND BLUE MAKES GREEN

If Nestorius was at fault for overemphasizing the two natures, then the next and last figure of controversy over Christ at

Chalcedon is guilty of overemphasizing the one person. In fact, Eutyches (378–454) ended up with a rather unique Christ. Eutyches was the archimandrite at Constantinople, which means that he ran the monastery and was just one notch below a bishop in the ecclesiastical hierarchy. To him Christ was a third thing (the Latin expression is *tertium quid*). The human and the divine natures conjoined in such a way as to create a new being. One new and different person fashioned out of two natures is how he liked to put it. That is a theological way of saying yellow and blue makes green. In the process, Eutyches compromised both the full humanity and the full deity of Christ. This was his way of avoiding the word/human or word/flesh debate altogether. His prescription, however, fared far, far worse than the disease. Flavian, bishop at Constantinople, could see the dangers in Eutyches and convened a synod that met at Constantinople in 448. The synod found Eutyches and his teachings out of bounds and condemned him and his followers.

## ROMAN EMPERORS AND THE COUNCIL OF CHALCEDON

**East**

| | |
|---|---|
| Theodosius II (408–450) | convened and supported the Council of Ephesus, 431, which condemned Nestorius; later supported Eutyches and deposed Flavian, the orthodox bishop of Constantinople, at the "Robber Council" in Ephesus, 449 |
| Marcian (450–457) | convened and supported decisions of the Council of Chalcedon, 451; enforced the decision of Chalcedon throughout the eastern empire |

**West**

| | |
|---|---|
| Valentinian III (429–455) | granted Leo supremacy over other bishops in the west in 444; supported and enforced the Council of Chalcedon's decisions in the west |

Eutyches and his followers, the Eutychians, knew a thing or two about politics, however. Eutyches had close ties with the imperial house of Theodosius II. Going through the emperor, Eutyches and his followers arranged for a "council" to meet at

Ephesus in 449. Leo the Great would come to call this synod a *latrocinium*, Latin for "robber council." This council reversed the decision against Eutyches and deposed Flavian as bishop. Eutyches's success, however, would be short-lived. In 450 Theodosius II died. A new emperor with a distinct taste for orthodoxy, Marcian, then ascended to power.

In 451 a new council convened by Marcian would deal the decisive blow to Eutychianism. Eutychianism made Christ something not fully human or fully divine at the incarnation, which means it made Christ something not fully human or fully divine at the cross. Once again the theologians on the side of orthodoxy made the connection between the doctrines of the incarnation and of the atonement. In the Chalcedonian Creed, which signaled the defeat of Eutyches, the key phrase from the Nicene Creed, that Christ is the God-man *"for us and for our salvation,"* would find a prominent place.

## 520 BISHOPS IN A ROOM

Chalcedon's achievement was nothing short of miraculous. The Council, called by Marcian, emperor in the east from 450–457, convened at Chalcedon in Asia Minor, just northwest of Constantinople and nestled on the shores of the Black Sea. Marcian had a political agenda—he could ill afford ecclesiastical division in the face of threats on the empire's eastern borders. The division in the church had come about through Marcian's predecessor, Theodosius II, whose lengthy rule in the east spanned from 408–450.

As mentioned above, Theodosius II clashed with Constantinople's bishop, Flavian, over Eutyches. Flavian's time as bishop would be rather short (446–449) but eventful. Flavian was the one who convened the synod at Constantinople in 448 that condemned Eutyches. Eutyches and his followers, through their connections with Theodosius II, arranged for the "Robber Council." With Theodosius II's blessing, Eutyches was restored and Flavian was deposed. Dioscorus, the bishop of Alexandria, presided over the "Robber Council." He dispatched an armed guard to pressure Flavian into signing the decision of the council. When Flavian refused, he was beaten so severely that a few days later he died. Even Leo's delegates were physically beaten.

Just before that "Robber Council" synod at Ephesus in 449, Leo, the bishop in Rome, sent Flavian a letter urging him to persevere against Eutyches. Leo, always the diplomat, also offered Flavian advice on how to proceed. The letter has come to be called Leo's "Tome." The word *tome* is usually reserved for a rather lengthy and weighty book. Leo's "Tome," at only about seven or so pages, finds its gravitas not in its size but in its theological rigor. Flavian asked that Leo's subordinates, two presbyters and a deacon who were there in support of Flavian, be permitted to read the letter. The bishops, under the influence of Theodosius II, rejected the letter outright and would not let the Roman contingent speak. The synod enraged onlookers. Theodosius II accomplished the reinstatement of Eutyches, but only at a cost of deep rifts in the church.

## CHALCEDON'S SCORECARD

| Good | Bad |
|---|---|
| Cyril of Alexandria | Apollinarius of Laodicea |
| Leo the Great of Rome | Nestorius of Constantinople |
| Flavian of Constantinople | Eutyches of Constantinople |
| | Dioscorus of Alexandria |

Theodosius II's death in the following year, 450, brought about a new set of circumstances for those for and against Eutyches. Marcian, the new emperor, desired the church's unity; so he convened a council at Chalcedon. While Leo was not present at the council, his letter, the "Tome," was, as were his subordinates, again the two presbyters and the deacon. His letter would come to be the decisive factor in the debates. Actually, merely five words from the letter would come to be the decisive factor. In the letter Leo relates Christ's human and divine nature by simply stating that Christ is "two natures in one person," a model of concision and precision.

The council met in five sessions during October 451. The first session overturned the synod at Ephesus in 449, the "Robber Council." In the process it excoriated Dioscorus, bishop of Alexandria, who dispatched the soldiers to beat the dissenting bishops of the "Robber Council." Despite his actions at the "Robber Council," Dioscorus was appointed to preside over the first session of Chalcedon. The decision of this first session not only put down Eutyches and exonerated Flavian, it also sent a clear message to Dioscorus. He was no longer the one calling the shots. In fact, after the first session Dioscorus went into hiding and refused to appear before the council again, even when summoned. The bishops meeting at session three of the Council of Chalcedon eventually excommunicated him, in absentia, and sent him into exile.

But not everyone in the room was happy with the decisions of the first session. Among the 520 bishops there would obviously be supporters of Eutyches and of Dioscorus. They would need some more convincing. Consequently, in its second session the council turned to drafting a statement of faith. This in and of itself turned out to be quite a challenge. There were two groups with opposing views of the nature of this confession. The first group consisted of those who had grown weary of the word/human and word/flesh debate between Antioch and Alexandria. They had grown weary of the intricacies of debating Apollinarianism, Nestorianism, and Eutychianism. This group simply did not want to engage the matter of relating the two natures of Christ. Instead all they wanted to do was to reaffirm the Nicene Creed, suspending the discussion of how the two natures come together. The second group disagreed. They saw the dangers in not trying to somehow express, in language true to Scripture, how the human and divine natures relate in Christ. If not dealt with decisively, this group argued, then even

110 || FOR US AND FOR OUR SALVATION

more complex and subtle views would keep popping up. Now was the time to deal with this issue and complete the trajectory started by Athanasius and the Nicene Council by offering a statement of the orthodox view of Christ's humanity and deity. It would take some work, this group acknowledged, but it was well worth the effort. The second group won out over the first, and the council pushed on.

By the fourth session the council was looking more and more to Leo's "Tome," setting the stage for the crucial fifth session held on October 22. This fifth session saw the writing and signing, by all 520 bishops, of the Chalcedonian Creed. (Mark your calendars: October 22 should be a day of celebration.) The creed starts off affirming Nicea before offering Leo's phrase, "two natures in one person." The Chalcedonian Creed inserts some significant phrases in between the first and second half of Leo's concise and precise statement. The creed affirms that Christ is:

> to be acknowledged in *two natures*, without confusion, without change, without division, without separation; the distinction of natures being by no means taken away by the union, but rather the property of each nature being preserved, and concurring in *one person* and one subsistence, not parted or divided in two persons, but one and the same Son, and only begotten, God the Word, the Lord Jesus Christ [emphasis added].

In affirming Christ as two natures in one person, the Creed repudiates directly and explicitly the teachings of Apollinarius, Eutyches, and Nestorius. Against Apollinarius, the Creed holds that the two natures are whole and intact in the one person. It denies that the divine nature, the *Logos*, replaced the human spirit in Christ. Instead, each nature was fully preserved. Against Nestorius, the Creed holds Christ to be two natures in one person without division or separation. It denies that Christ is two persons, two "he's." Finally, against Eutyches, the Creed declares the two natures not to be confused and changed but rather declares that the distinction of the two natures remains fully intact without any alteration.

The intervening phrases have not made their way into the history of the Christian tradition. But the phrase "two natures in one person" certainly has. Another phrase from Chalcedon has become a fixture for orthodox Christianity. Chalcedon adds that Christ is not only one person but also *one subsistence*. The Greek word is *hypostasis*; the Latin word is *subsistantiam*. Theologians use this Greek word in speaking of the "hypostatic union." This term refers to the unity of the two natures in Christ. While Christ is two natures, fully human and fully divine, he is simultaneously one person or one being. The term *hypostasis* functioned synonymously with the word for "substance" in Greek philosophy. It may be recalled from Chapter 1 that "substance" stood for that which is essential to a thing, that which makes something what it is.

Why did Chalcedon choose to use this word and potentially entangle itself in philosophical discussions? The answer may simply be that Chalcedon was going out of its way to stress the two natures, while at the same time going out of its way to stress the unity of the one person. It used the term *person* (*prosopon* in Greek; *personam* in Latin), the common term that everyone would have understood. And it used the term *hypostasis*, the term that the learned would understand and recognize at once in its implication and weight. The bishops at Chalcedon did not want anyone leaving the council, or anyone in the church for that matter, without fully understanding what they were saying about Christ. They wanted no misunderstanding in terms of what they were accepting as orthodoxy and rejecting as heresy.

We may not always understand or even immediately appreciate the precise and technical language theologians use to express what the Bible teaches on any given subject. And to be sure, sometimes theologians can exercise their gift for making the simple and clear complex and obtuse. At times, however, the situation demands precise and technical vocabulary. The bishops gathered at Chalcedon were not looking to make the clear complex, nor were they desirous of alienating the untrained laity in the church. The heresies that they were contending with had blurred the lines of orthodoxy and what had been accepted at Nicea. The heretics had cleverly shaped and molded their teaching to coincide with some biblical texts and to, at least in part, sound plausible. In light of this situation, Chalcedon needed to stake out the boundaries with precision. And that it did.

The hypostatic union may require some careful explaining, but it is a phrase and a belief that must not be brushed aside as merely technical vocabulary for the professionals. The hypostatic union, and what it means, belongs to the church. This two-nature-in-one-person Christology, the hypostatic union, merits a deeper look.

## NOT TWO, NOT ONE, BUT TWO IN ONE

There are advantages to the view of Nestorius, that Christ is so much two natures that he verges close to being two persons. There are also advantages to the view of Eutyches, that Christ is a singular, new kind of being or person altogether. It's hard for us to imagine the divine being conjoined with a human being that is born and undergoes development and growth, not to mention death on the cross for sin. Surely there are perplexities in seeing the two natures simultaneously. And it lies well beyond comprehension to explain exactly how the two natures do come together. If Nestorius and Eutyches provide a way out of this labyrinth, then their views may warrant attention. But the reality is that neither view provides such a way out. Instead they each, in their own way, take us further into the labyrinth.

The Chalcedonian Creed is important not only for what it says, but also for what it doesn't even try to say. It avoids trying to explain how the two natures come together; it just states that they do. It avoids trying to solve perplexities raised by the union of the human and divine natures. Instead it declares that Christ is fully and entirely both, while at the same time one person. Leo would say in one of his sermons, "We should not be disturbed but rather strengthened by these mysteries." Chalcedon recognized that when you're dealing with the person of Christ, you're dealing with a mystery. Many centuries after Chalcedon, Dietrich Bonhoeffer would also be stunned by this mystery, declaring, "The child in the manger is wholly God."[6]

Yet Chalcedon also recognized that when you're dealing with the person of Christ, you're dealing with the biblical material about him. What Chalcedon declares, consequently, carefully navigates affirming what the Bible teaches without going beyond what the Bible teaches.

It was vital, however, for it to affirm what the Bible teaches about Christ. The problem with stressing the two natures without the counterbalance of the one person, as Nestorius does, is that Christ becomes a conflicted individual. The problem with stressing the unity without the counterbalance of the two intact natures, as Eutyches does, is that Christ loses his human and divine identity. As such, he is not truly our representative. The Christ of Eutyches falls way short of Paul's teaching of Christ as the last Adam (Rom. 5:12-21; 1 Cor. 15:42-49).

Despite its contradiction to Scripture, Eutychianism had a way of hanging on in the church. Eutychianism belongs to a larger category of heresy called *monophysitism*. As we have seen, the Greek word *physos* means "nature," and *mono* means "one." This view holds that Christ is one unified nature, not two natures. Apollinarius was knocking on the door of this heresy when he taught that the divine *Logos* replaced the human spirit in Christ. Eutyches ran right through the door when he proposed Christ to be a new being altogether. After Chalcedon, monophysitism continued to have a hold in pockets throughout the church.

The fifth ecumenical council, Constantinople II, held in 553, actually teetered on the edge of taking the church away from the stance of Chalcedon (two natures in one person) by leaning toward monophysitism. This council spawned a new version of monophysitism, known as monotheletism. This view holds that Christ had one unified will, the divine will. *Theles* is the Greek word for "will." The sixth ecumenical council, Constantinople III, held in 680, declared this view heretical. Stressing once again the teachings of Chalcedon that Jesus is fully and truly two natures, this council added that Jesus possessed two wills, one human and one divine. By now the council had to use the terms *dyophysotism* (two natures) and *dyotheletism* (two wills). As the heresies became more subtle and complex, orthodox theologians responded in kind.

What becomes evident in all of these heresies is the stumbling block and scandal of the person of Christ. There was still a great deal of Platonism going around in the fifth and following centuries, enough Platonism at least to cause some theologians to shrink back from seeing Christ's full humanity. Instead they concocted rather sophisticated schemes to avoid taking Christ as he comes in his incarnation and as Scripture presents him—as fully human, as a babe lying in a manger. Again, the church of today can be thankful that there were those who both recognized the problems with these heretical views and had the wherewithal to do something about them. Leo, in his famous "Tome," explains why.

## FOR US AND FOR OUR SALVATION

Leo held that Christ had to be fully and truly human "for the paying off of the debt belonging to our condition." Christ "repaired" that which was broken in his creatures by becoming one of us. Leo carefully maintains that Christ did not share in our sin. He has Christ "partaking of our weaknesses," but not of our faults; Christ "took the form of a slave without stain of sin." Any compromise in Christ's full humanity threatened Christ's work of redemption. Leo put it pointedly: "We should not be able to make use of the Conqueror's victory, if it had been won outside our nature."[7]

Leo not only drove this theme home in his many letters—he also preached it in his sermons. Scholars have identified 123 extant letters and ninety-six extant sermons from the pen of Leo, with more of his writings simply lost to history. Throughout his sermons he underscored the necessity of holding firm to the creeds and avoiding heresies. And he told his congregation that their belief had everything to do with their living the Christian life. "This belief in the Lord's incarnation, dearly beloved," Leo preached, "hold firm with heart unshaken and abstain from all the lies of the heretics, and remember that your works of mercy will only then profit you, and your strict continence only then bear fruit, when your minds are unsoiled by any defilement from wrong opinions." He also shows how the orthodox view of Christ is the only view that makes sense of Scripture. Many of his sermons follow the cycle of the liturgical calendar. Those dealing with the Advent and Easter seasons overflow with references to his two-nature, one-person Christology. For Leo, the incarnation, the temptation, Jesus' public ministry, passion week, the cross, and the resurrection all must be seen through the lens of the two natures in one person.[8]

The truths of the incarnation, Leo heralded, never suffer from being repeated. Consequently, he endeavored to ensure that the church would embrace the truth of the incarnation—namely, that Christ as fully God took on flesh and became fully human. In Leo's thinking, a proper view of the incarnation leads to a proper view of the atonement. The reverse also happens to be true. "Estimate this atonement at its right worth," Leo warns. Failing to see Christ as the God-man diminishes the worth of the atonement.[9]

Leo also preached on how fitting the humanity of Christ is to his task of redemption. He observes that Christ "has taken on him the nature of man, thereby to reconcile it to its Author: in order that the inventor of death, the devil, might be conquered through that nature which he had conquered." Christ's humanity accomplishes two purposes here—restoring humanity to its Creator and toppling Satan in the very arena where he thought himself to be victorious. On this latter point Leo further observes, "And in this conflict undertaken for us, the fight was fought on great and wondrous principles of fairness; for the Almighty Lord enters the lists [arenas] with his savage foe not in his own majesty but in our humility."[10]

It's not just Christ's humanity, however, that gives his work on the cross its significance. His deity also comes into play. Leo weaves the two together in the following selection from a sermon in which he uses much of his own language from the "Tome," the famous letter to Flavian. He declares that Christ,

> with the purpose of delivering man from eternal death, became man: so bending himself to take on Him our humility without decrease in his own majesty, that remaining what he was and assuming what he was not, he might unite the true form of a slave to that form in which he is equal to God the Father, and join both natures together in such a compact that the lower should not be swallowed up in its exaltation nor the higher impaired by its new associate.

Leo then relates the union of these two natures to Christ's death on the cross:

> Without detriment therefore to the properties of either substance which then came together in one person, majesty took on humility, strength weakness, eternity mortality; and for the paying off of the debt belonging to our condition, inviolable nature was united with passible nature, and true God and true man were combined to form one Lord, so that, as suits the needs of our case, one and the same Mediator between God and man, the man Christ Jesus, could both die with the one and rise again with the other.[11]

Christ as the God-man accomplished redemption. Christ, Leo declared with wisdom and courage in the face of great controversy, was the God-man for us and for our salvation.

## CONCLUSION

Though further controversy would come in the church, the fifth century, and especially the Council of Chalcedon in 451, went a long way in settling the church's theology of the person of Christ. The Chalcedonian Creed left little room for improvement. Indeed, the phrase *two natures in one person* has enjoyed a lasting legacy in the history of the Christian tradition, as has the theological phrase *hypostatic union*. Later theologians, especially Anselm (1033–1109) and the Reformers of the sixteenth century, would fully develop the doctrine of the work of Christ, building entirely on the doctrine of the person of Christ hammered out by these early church fathers. Even in the early fathers we can see that they were making the connection between the person and work of Christ. They knew that Christ was the God-man at the incarnation in Bethlehem and in his atonement on the cross. They knew that Christ was the God-man for us and for our salvation.

Many of these church fathers have lapsed from the collective memory of today's church. Gone are the names of Leo and Flavian. Foggy is the memory of the work of the bishops at Chalcedon. Yet, the church today reflexively draws upon them and their work when it thinks of the person of Christ. It might further benefit the church to clear away some of the fog concerning their legacy. We should know of Leo and his wisdom and courage. We should know of Flavian and his sacrifice of his very life. Not because Leo and Flavian should be exalted, but because they so well articulated Christ and his sacrifice for us and for our salvation.

## CHAPTER SIX

# In Their Own Words:
## Select Documents from the
## Fifth Century

The Council of Chalcedon (451) stands at the end of four long centuries of controversy concerning the person of Christ. This is not to say that heresies and problems concerning the person of Christ came to an end at this council. Rather, it is to say that the "Definition" or Creed of Chalcedon offers a full and exacting summary of the biblical teaching concerning the deity and humanity of Christ. Chalcedon crystallizes the mass of material about Christ by declaring him to be two natures, fully God and fully human, conjoined in one person. The readings below reveal the origin of this phrase to be in the sermons and letters of Leo, bishop of Rome. Readings from the proceedings of the Council of Chalcedon are also included. Conspicuously absent from the discussions at Chalcedon is Augustine's work. He had died in 430, but his shadow was cast over just about every discussion in the early church. He had much to say about the person of Christ, including his written works against Arianism. He was also one of the most formative writers on the Trinity. A brief selection from his *On Christian Doctrine* concerning Christ starts off these selections.

## AUGUSTINE (354-430)

In this selection from *On Christian Doctrine*, Augustine artfully declares how Christ as the God-man provides the only way to salvation, thus linking the person of Christ with the work of Christ.

*Augustine, On Christian Doctrine (De Doctrina Christiana), Book I, Chapter 34; date: 426; source: Nicene and Post-Nicene Fathers, First Series, Vol. II (Grand Rapids, MI: Eerdmans, 1957), 532.*

And mark that even when He who is Himself the Truth and the Word, by whom all things were made, had been made flesh that He might dwell among us, the apostle yet says: "Yea, though we have known Christ after the flesh, yet now henceforth know we Him no more." For Christ, desiring not only to give the possession to those who had completed the journey, but also to be Himself the way to those who were just setting out, determined to take a fleshly body. Whence also that expression, "The Lord created me in the beginning of His way," that is, that those who wished to come might begin their journey in Him. The apostle, therefore, although still on the way, and following after God who called him to the reward of His heavenly calling, yet forgetting those things which were behind, and pressing on towards those things which were before, had already passed over the beginning of the way, and had now no further need of it; yet by this way all must commence their journey who desire to attain to the truth, and to rest in eternal life. For He says: "I am the way, and the truth, and the life;" that is, by me men come, to me they come, in me they rest. For when we come to Him, we come to the Father also, because through an equal an equal is known; and the Holy Spirit binds, and as it were seals us, so that we are able to rest permanently in the supreme and unchangeable God. And hence we may learn how essential it is that nothing should detain us on the way, when not even our Lord Himself, so far as He has condescended to be our way, is willing to detain us, but wishes us rather to press on; and, instead of weakly clinging to temporal things, even though these have been put on and worn by Him for our salvation, to pass over them quickly, and to struggle to attain unto Himself, who has freed our nature from the bondage of temporal things, and has set it down at the right hand of His Father.

## LEO (B. ?-D. 461)

The most significant figure leading up to and during the Council of Chalcedon was not even present at the council. His thoughts were, however. His so-called "Tome," a reply to a letter from Flavian concerning Eutyches, provided the theological substance of the work of the 520 bishops gathered at Chalcedon. Leo further made sure that those under his care in Rome knew full well the biblical teaching of the person of Christ and its consequences. In a series of sermons to coincide with the Feast of the Nativity in the liturgical calendar, Leo persuasively argued for the orthodox view of Christ. Selections from three of these sermons are included. In order to set the stage for his "Tome," the letter that Flavian sent to Leo is also included. The "Tome" is reproduced in full.

*Letter from Flavian to Leo; date: 448; source: Nicene and Post-Nicene Fathers, Second Series, Vol. XII (Grand Rapids, MI: Eerdmans, 1957), 34-35.*

To the most holy and God-loving father and fellow-bishop, Leo, Flavian, greeting in the Lord.

I: There is nothing which can stay the devil's wickedness, that "restless evil, full of deadly poison." Above and below it "goes about," seeking "whom it may" strike, dismay, and "devour." Whence to watch, to be sober unto prayer, to draw near to God, to eschew foolish questionings, to follow the fathers and not to go beyond the eternal bounds, this we have learnt from Holy Writ. And so I give up the excess of grief and abundant tears over the capture of one of the clergy who are under me, and whom I could not save nor snatch from the wolf, although I was ready to lay down my life for him. How was he caught, how did he leap away, hating the voice of the caller and turning aside also from the memory of the Fathers and thoroughly detesting their paths. And thus I proceed with my account.

II: There are some "in sheep's clothing, but inwardly they are ravening wolves:" whom we know by their fruit. These men seem indeed at first to be of us, but they are not of us: "for if they had been of us, they would no doubt have continued with us." But when they have spewed out their impiety, throwing out the guile that is in them, and seizing the weaker ones, and those who have their senses unpracticed in the divine utterances, they carry them along with themselves to destruction, wresting and doing despite to the Fathers' doctrines, just as they do the Holy Scriptures also to their own destruction: whom we must be forewarned of and take heed lest some should be misled by their wickedness and shaken in their firmness. "For they have sharpened their tongues like serpents: adder's poison is under their lips," as the prophet has cried out about them.

III: Such a one, therefore, has now shown himself amongst us, Eutyches,[1] for many years a presbyter and archimandrite, pretending to hold the same belief as ours, and to have the right Faith in him: indeed he resists the blasphemy of Nestorius, and feigns a controversy with him, but the exposition of the Faith composed by the 318 holy fathers,[2] and the letter that Cyril[3] of holy memory wrote to Nestorius, and one by the same author on the same subject to the Easterns, these writings, to which all have given their assent, he has tried to upset, and revive the old evil dogmas of the blasphemous Valentinus and Apollinarius. He has not feared the warning of the True King: "Whoso shall cause one of the least of these little ones to stumble, it was better that a millstone should be hanged about his neck, and that he should be sunk in the depth of the sea." But casting away all shame, and shaking off the cloak which covered his error, he openly in our holy synod persisted in saying that our Lord Jesus Christ ought not to be understood by us as having two natures after His incarnation in one substance and in one person: nor yet that the Lord's flesh was of the same substance with us, as if assumed from us and united to God the Word hypostatically: but he said that the Virgin who bare him was indeed of the same substance with us according to the flesh, but the Lord Himself did not assume from her flesh of the same substance with us: but the Lord's body was not a man's body, although that which issued from the Virgin was a human body, resisting all the expositions of the holy Fathers.[4]

IV: But not to make my letter too long by detailing everything, we have sent your holiness the proceedings which some time since we took in the matter: therein we deprived him as convicted on these charges, of his priesthood, of the management of his monastery and of our communion: in order that your holiness also knowing the facts of his case may make his wickedness manifest to all the God-loving bishops who are under your reverence; lest perchance if they do not know the views which he holds, and of which he has been openly convicted, they may be found to be in correspondence with him as a fellow-believer by letter or by other means. I and those who are with me give much greeting to you and to all the brotherhood in Christ. The Lord keep you in safety and prayer for us, O most God-Loving Father.

*Leo, The "Tome," Letter 28, to Flavian; date: 449; source: Nicene and Post-Nicene Fathers, Second Series, Vol. XII, 38–43.*

I: Having read your letter, beloved, at the late arrival of which we are surprised, and having perused the detailed account of the bishops' acts, we have at last found out what the scandal was which had arisen among you against the purity of the Faith: and what before seemed concealed has now been unlocked and laid open to our view: from which it is shown that Eutyches, who used to seem worthy of all respect in virtue of his priestly office, is very unwary and exceedingly ignorant, so that it is even of him that the prophet has said: "he refused to understand so as to do well: he thought upon iniquity in his bed." But what more iniquitous than to hold blasphemous opinions, and not to give way to those who are wiser and more learned than ourself. Now into this unwisdom fall they who, finding themselves hindered from knowing the truth by some obscurity, have recourse not to the prophets' utterances, not to the Apostles' letters, nor to the injunctions of the Gospel but to their own selves: and thus they stand out as masters of error because they were never disciples of truth. For what learning has he acquired about the pages of the New and Old Testament, who has not even grasped the rudiments of the [Nicene] Creed? And that which, throughout the world, is professed by the mouth of every one who is to be born again, is not yet taken in by the heart of this old man.

II: Not knowing, therefore, what he was bound to think concerning the incarnation of the Word of God, and not wishing to gain the light of knowledge by researches through the length and breadth of the Holy Scriptures, he might at least have listened attentively to that general and uniform confession, whereby the whole body of the faithful confess that they *believe in God the Father Almighty, and in Jesus Christ, His only Son, our Lord, who was born of the Holy Spirit and the Virgin Mary.* By which three statements the devices of almost all heretics are overthrown. For not only is God believed to be both Almighty and the Father, but the Son is shown to be co-eternal with Him, differing in nothing from the Father because He is *God from God*, Almighty from Almighty, and being born from the Eternal one is co-eternal with Him; not later in point of time, not lower in power, not unlike in glory, not divided in essence: but at the same time the only begotten of the eternal Father was born eternal of the Holy Spirit and the Virgin Mary. And this nativity which took place in time took nothing from, and added nothing to that divine and eternal birth, but expended itself wholly on the restoration of man who had been deceived: in order that he might both vanquish death and overthrow by his strength, the Devil who possessed the power of death. For we should not now be able to overcome the author of sin and death unless He

took our nature on Him and made it His own, whom neither *our nature is essential*
sin could pollute nor death retain. Doubtless then, He was conceived of the Holy Spirit within the womb of His Virgin Mother,
who brought Him forth without the loss of her virginity) even
as she conceived Him without its loss.

But if he could not draw a rightful understanding of the
matter from this pure source of the Christian belief, because
he had darkened the brightness of the clear truth by a veil of
blindness peculiar to himself, he might have submitted himself
to the teaching of the Gospels. And when Matthew speaks of
"the Book of the Generation of Jesus Christ, the Son of David,
the Son of Abraham," He might have also sought out the
instruction afforded by the statements of the Apostles. And
reading in the Epistle to the Romans, "Paul, a servant of Jesus
Christ, called an Apostle, separated unto the Gospel of God,
which He had promised before by His prophets in the Holy
Scripture concerning His son, who was made unto Him of the
seed of David after the flesh," he might have bestowed a loyal
carefulness upon the pages of the prophets. And finding the
promise of God who says to Abraham, "In thy seed shall all
nations be blest," to avoid all doubt as to the reference of this
seed, he might have followed the Apostle when He says, "To
Abraham were the promises made and to his seed. He says not
and to seeds, as if in many, but as if in one, and to thy seed which
is Christ." Isaiah's prophecy also he might have grasped by a
closer attention to what he says, "Behold, a virgin shall conceive
and bear a Son and they shall call His name Immanuel," which
is interpreted "God with us." And the same prophet's words he
might have read faithfully. "A child is born to us, a Son is given
to us, whose power is upon His shoulder, and they shall call His
name the Angel of the Great Counsel, Wonderful, Counselor,
the Mighty God, the Prince of Peace, the Father of the age to
come." And then he would not speak so erroneously as to say
that the Word became flesh in such a way that Christ, born of
the Virgin's womb, had the form of man, but had not the reality

of His mother's body. Or is it possible that he thought our Lord Jesus Christ was not of our nature for this reason, that the angel, who was sent to the blessed Mary ever Virgin, says, "The Holy Ghost shall come upon thee and the power of the Most High shall overshadow thee: and therefore that Holy Thing also that shall be born of thee shall be called the Son of God," on the supposition that as the conception of the Virgin was a Divine act, the flesh of the conceived did not partake of the conceiver's nature? But that birth so uniquely wondrous and so wondrously unique, is not to be understood in such wise that the properties of His kind were removed through the novelty of His creation. For though the Holy Spirit imparted fertility to the Virgin, yet a real body was received from her body; and, "Wisdom building her a house," "the Word became flesh and dwelled among us," that is, in that flesh which he took from man and which he quickened with the breath of a higher life.

III: Without detriment therefore to the properties of either nature and substance which then came together in one person,[5] majesty took on humility, strength weakness, eternity mortality: and for the paying off of the debt belonging to our condition inviolable nature was united with possible nature, so that, as suited the needs of our case, one and the same Mediator between God and men, the Man Christ Jesus, could both die with the one and not die with the other. Thus in the whole and perfect nature of true man was true God born, complete in what was His own, complete in what was ours. And by "ours" we mean what the Creator formed in us from the beginning and what He undertook to repair. For what the Deceiver brought in and man deceived committed, had no trace in the Savior. Nor, because He partook of man's weaknesses, did He therefore share our faults. He took the form of a slave without stain of sin, increasing the human and not diminishing the divine: because that emptying of Himself whereby the Invisible made Himself visible and, Creator and Lord of all things though He be, wished to be a mortal, was the bending down of pity, not the failing of power. Accordingly He who while remaining in the form of God made man, was also made man in the form of a slave. For both natures retain their own proper character without loss: and as the form of God did not do away with the form of a slave, so the form of a slave did not impair the form of God. For inasmuch as the Devil used to boast that man had been cheated by his guile into losing the divine gifts, and bereft of the boon of immortality had undergone sentence of death, and that he had found some solace in his troubles from having a partner in delinquency, and that God also at the demand of the principle of justice had changed His own purpose towards man whom He had created in such honor: there was need for the issue of a secret counsel, that the unchangeable God whose will cannot be robbed of its own kindness, might carry out the first design of His Fatherly care towards us by a more hidden mystery; and that man who had been driven into his fault by the treacherous cunning of the devil might not perish contrary to the purpose of God.

IV: There enters then these lower parts of the world the Son of God, descending from His heavenly home and yet not quitting His Father's glory, begotten in a new order by a new nativity. In a new order, because being invisible in His own nature, He became visible in ours, and He whom nothing could contain was content to be contained: abiding before all time He began to be in time: the Lord of all things, He obscured His immeasurable majesty and took on Him the form of a servant: being God that cannot suffer, He did not disdain to be man that can, and, immortal as He is, to subject Himself to the laws of death. The Lord assumed His mother's nature without her faultiness: nor in the Lord Jesus Christ, born of the Virgin's womb, does the wonderfulness of His birth make His nature unlike ours. For He who is true God is also true man: and in this union there is no lie, since the humility of manhood and the loftiness of the Godhead both meet there. For as God is not changed by the showing of pity, so man is not swallowed up by the dignity. For each form does what is proper

to it with the co-operation of the other; that is the Word per-
forming what appertains to the Word, and the flesh carrying out
what appertains to the flesh. One of them sparkles with miracles,
the other succumbs to injuries. And as the Word does not cease
to be on an equality with His Father's glory, so the flesh does
not forego the nature of our race. For it must again and again
be repeated that one and the same is truly Son of God and truly
son of man.[6] God in that "in the beginning was the Word, and
the Word was with God, and the Word was God;" man in that
"the Word became flesh and dwelt in us." God in that "all things
were made by Him, and without Him was nothing made":
man in that "He was made of a woman, made under law." The
nativity of the flesh was the manifestation of human nature: the
childbearing of a virgin is the proof of Divine power. The infancy
of a babe is shown in the humbleness of its cradle: the greatness
of the Most High is proclaimed by the angels' voices. He whom
Herod treacherously endeavors to destroy is like ourselves in
our earliest stage: but He whom the Magi delight to worship
on their knees is the Lord of all. So too when He came to the
baptism of John, His forerunner, lest He should not be known
through the veil of flesh which covered His Divinity, the Father's
voice thundering from the sky, said, "This is My beloved Son,
in whom I am well pleased." And thus Him whom the devil's
craftiness attacks as man, the ministries of angels serve as God.
To be hungry and thirsty, to be weary, and to sleep, is clearly
human: but to satisfy 5,000 men with five loaves, and to bestow
on the woman of Samaria living water, draughts of which can
secure the drinker from thirsting any more, to walk upon the
surface of the sea with feet that do not sink, and to quell the ris-
ings of the waves by rebuking the winds, is, without any doubt,
Divine. Just as therefore, to pass over many other instances, it
is not part of the same nature to be moved to tears of pity for a
dead friend, and when the stone that closed the four-days' grave
was removed, to raise that same friend to life with a voice of
command: or, to hang on the cross, and turning day to night, to

make all the elements tremble: or, to be pierced with nails, and yet open the gates of paradise to the robber's faith: so it is not part of the same nature to say, "I and the Father are one," and to say, "the Father is greater than I." For although in the Lord Jesus Christ God and man is one person, yet the source of the degradation, which is shared by both, is one, and the source of the glory, which is shared by both, is another. For His manhood, which is less than the Father, comes from our side: His Godhead, which is equal to the Father, comes from the Father.

V: Therefore in consequence of this unity of person which is to be understood in both natures, we read of the Son of Man also descending from heaven, when the Son of God took flesh from the Virgin who bore Him. And again the Son of God is said to have been crucified and buried, although it was not actually in His Divinity whereby the Only-begotten is co-eternal and con-substantial with the Father, but in His weak human nature that He suffered these things. And so it is that in the Creed also we all confess that the Only-begotten Son of God was crucified and buried, according to that saying of the Apostle: "for if they had known, they would never have crucified the Lord of glory." But when our Lord and Savior Himself would instruct His disciples' faith by His questionings, He said, "Whom do men say that I, the Son of Man, am?" And when they had put on record the various opinions of other people, He said, "But you, whom do you say that I am?" I, that is, who am the Son of Man, and whom you see in the form of a slave, and in true flesh, whom do you say that I am? Whereupon he blessed Peter, whose divinely inspired confession was destined to profit all nations, [who] said, "Thou art Christ, the Son of the living God." And not undeservedly was he pronounced blessed by the Lord, drawing from the chief corner-stone the solidity of power which his name also expresses, he, who, through the revelation of the Father, confessed Him to be at once Christ and Son of God: because the receiving of the one of these without the other was of no avail to salvation, and it was equally perilous to have believed the Lord Jesus Christ to be either only God without man, or only man without God. But after the Lord's resurrection—which, of course, was of His true body, because He was raised the same as He had died and been buried—what else was effected by the forty days' delay than the cleansing of our faith's purity from all darkness? For to that end He talked with His disciples, and dwelt and ate with them, He allowed Himself to be handled with diligent and curious touch by those who were affected by doubt, He entered when the doors were shut upon the Apostles, and by His breathing upon them gave them the Holy Spirit, and bestowing on them the light of understanding, opened the secrets of the Holy Scriptures. So again He showed the wound in His side, the marks of the nails, and all the signs of His quite recent suffering, saying, "See My hands and feet, that it is I. Handle Me and see that a spirit hath not flesh and bones, as ye see Me have;" in order that the properties of His Divine and human nature might be acknowledged to remain still inseparable: and that we might know the Word not to be different from the flesh, in such a sense as also to confess that the one Son of God is both the Word and flesh. Of this mystery of the faith your opponent Eutyches must be reckoned to have but little sense if he but recognized our nature in the Only-begotten of God neither through the humiliation of His having to die, nor through the glory of His rising again. Nor has he any fear of the blessed apostle and evangelist John's declaration when he says, "every spirit which confesses Jesus Christ to have come in the flesh, is of God: and every spirit which destroys Jesus is not of God, and this is Antichrist." But what is "to destroy Jesus," except to take away the human nature from Him, and to render void the mystery, by which alone we were saved, by the most barefaced fictions. The truth is that being in darkness about the nature of Christ's body, he must also be befooled by the same blindness in the matter of His sufferings. For if he does not think the cross of the Lord fictitious, and does not doubt that the punishment He underwent to save the world is likewise true, let him acknowledge the flesh of Him whose death he already believes: and let him not disbelieve Him man with a body like ours, since he acknowledges Him to have been able to suffer: seeing that the denial of His true flesh is also the denial of His bodily suffering. If therefore he receives the Christian faith, and does not turn away his ears from the preaching of the Gospel: let him see what was the nature that hung pierced with nails on the wooden cross, and, when the side of the Crucified was opened by the soldier's spear, let him understand whence it was that blood and water flowed, that the Church of God might be watered from the font and from the cup. Let him hear also the blessed Apostle Peter, proclaiming that the sanctification of the Spirit takes place through the sprinkling of Christ's blood. And let him not read cursorily the same Apostle's words when he says, "Knowing that not with corruptible things, such as silver and gold, have ye been redeemed from your vain manner of life which is part of your fathers' tradition, but with the precious blood of Jesus Christ as of a lamb without spot and blemish." Let him not resist too the witness of the blessed Apostle John, who says: "and the blood of Jesus the Son of God cleanses us from all sin." And again: "this is the victory which overcomes the world, our faith." And "who is He that overcomes the world save He that believeth that Jesus is the Son of God. This is He that came by water and blood, Jesus Christ: not by water only, but by water and blood. And it is the Spirit that testifies, because the Spirit is the truth, because there are three that bear witness, the Spirit, the water and the blood, and the three are one." The Spirit, that is, of sanctification, and the blood of redemption, and the water of baptism: because the three are one, and remain undivided, and none of them is separated from this connection; because the catholic Church lives and progresses by this faith, so that in Christ Jesus neither the manhood without the true Godhead nor the Godhead without the true manhood is believed in.

VI: But when during your cross-examination Eutyches

replied and said, "I confess that our Lord had two natures before the union but after the union I confess but one,"[7] I am surprised that so absurd and mistaken a statement of his should not have been criticized and rebuked by his judges, and that an utterance which reaches the height of stupidity and blasphemy should be allowed to pass as if nothing offensive had been heard: for the impiety of saying that the Son of God was of two natures before His incarnation is only equaled by the iniquity of asserting that there was but one nature in Him after "the Word became flesh." And to the end that Eutyches may not think this a right or defensible opinion because it was not contradicted by any expression of yourselves, we warn you, beloved brother, to take anxious care that if ever through the inspiration of God's mercy the case is brought to a satisfactory conclusion, his ignorant mind be purged from this pernicious idea as well as others. He was, indeed, just beginning to beat a retreat from his erroneous conviction, as the order of proceedings shows, insofar as when hemmed in by your remonstrances he agreed to say what he had not said before and to acquiesce in that belief to which before he had been opposed. However, when he refused to give his consent to the anathematizing of his blasphemous dogma, you understood, brother, that he abode by his treachery and deserved to receive a verdict of condemnation. And yet, if he grieves over it faithfully and to good purpose, and, late though it be, acknowledges how rightly the bishops' authority has been set in motion; or if with his own mouth and hand in your presence he recants his wrong opinions, no mercy that is shown to him when penitent can be found fault with: because our Lord, that true and "good shepherd" who laid down His life for His sheep and who came to save not lose men's souls, wishes us to imitate His kindness; in order that while justice constrains us when we sin, mercy may prevent our rejection when we have returned. For then at last is the true Faith most profitably defended when a false belief is condemned even by the supporters of it.

Now for the loyal and faithful execution of the whole matter, we have appointed to represent us our brothers Julius, Bishop and Renatus, priest, as well as my son Hilary, deacon.[8] And with them we have associated Dulcitius, our notary, whose faith is well approved: being sure that the Divine help will be given us, so that he who had erred may be saved when the wrongness of his view has been condemned. God keep you safe, beloved brother.

The 13th of June, 449, in the consulship of the most illustrious Asturius and Protogenes.

*Leo, Letter CXXIV, To the Monks of Palestine; date: ?; source: Nicene*
*and Post-Nicene Fathers, Second Series, Vol. XII, 93-94.*

VI: Although therefore from that beginning whereby in the Virgin's womb "the Word became flesh," no sort of division ever arose between the Divine and the human substance, and through all the growth and changes of His body, the actions were of one Person the whole time, yet we do not by any mixing of them up confound those very acts which were done inseparably: and from the character of the acts we perceive what belonged to either form.[9] For neither do His Divine acts affect His human, nor His human acts His Divine, since both  concur in this way and to this very end that in their operation His twofold qualities be not absorbed the one by the other, nor His individuality doubled) Therefore let those Christian phantom-mongers tell us, what nature of the Savior's it was that was fastened to the wood of the Cross, that lay in the tomb, and that on the third day rose in the flesh when the stone was rolled away from the grave: or what kind of body Jesus presented to His disciples' eyes entering when the doors were shut upon them: seeing that to drive away the beholders' disbelief, He required them to inspect with their eyes and to handle with their hands the still open prints of the nails and the flesh wound of His pierced side. But if in spite of the truth being so clear, their persistence in heresy will not abandon their position in the darkness, let them show whence they promise themselves the hope of eternal life, which no one can attain to, save through the mediator between God and man, the man Jesus Christ. For, "There is not another name given to men under heaven, in which they must be saved." Neither is there any ransoming of men from captivity, save in His blood, "who gave Himself a ransom for all": who, as the blessed apostle proclaims, "when He was in the form of God, thought it not robbery that He was equal with God; but emptied Himself, receiving the form of a slave, being made in the likeness of men, and being found in fashion as a man He humbled Himself, being made obedient even unto death, the death of the cross. For which reason God also exalted Him, and gave Him a name which is above every name: that in the name of Jesus every knee may bow of things in heaven, of things on the earth, and of things under the earth, and that every tongue may confess that the Lord Jesus Christ is in the glory of God the Father."[10]

*Leo, Sermon XXIII, "On the Feast of the Nativity, III," Section 3; date: c. 440–445; source: Nicene and Post-Nicene Fathers, Second Series, Vol. XII, 133.*

III: In order therefore that we might be called to eternal bliss from our original bond and from earthly errors, He came down Himself to us to Whom we could not ascend, because, although there was in many the love of truth, yet the variety of our shifting opinions was deceived by the craft of misleading demons, and man's ignorance was dragged into diverse and conflicting notions by a falsely-called science. But to remove this mockery, whereby men's minds were taken captive to serve the arrogant devil, the teaching of the Law was not sufficient, nor could our nature be restored merely by the Prophets' exhortations; but the reality of redemption had to be added to moral injunctions, and our fundamentally corrupt origin had to be re-born afresh. A Victim had to be offered for our atonement Who should be both

a partner of our race and free from our contamination, so that
this design of God whereby it pleased Him to take away the sin
of the world in the Nativity and Passion of Jesus Christ, might
reach to all generations: and that we should not be disturbed
but rather strengthened by these mysteries, which vary with the
character of the times, since the Faith, whereby we live, has at
no time suffered variation.

*Leo, Sermon XXVIII, "On the Feast of the Nativity, VIII,"*
*Sections 5-7, 143-144.*

V: There are many other astounding falsehoods also which
we must not weary your ears, beloved, with enumerating. But
after all these various impieties, which are closely connected
by the relationship that exists between one form of blasphemy
and another, we call your devout attention to the avoiding of
these two errors in particular: one of which, with Nestorius
for its author, some time ago attempted to gain ground, but
ineffectually; the other, which is equally damnable, has more
recently sprung up with Eutyches as its propounder. The former dared to maintain that the blessed Virgin Mary was the
mother of Christ's manhood only, so that in her conception
and childbearing no union might be believed to have taken
place of the Word and the Flesh: because the Son of God did
not Himself become Son of Man, but of His mere condescen-
sion linked Himself with created man. This can in no wise
be tolerated by catholic ears, which are so imbued with the
gospel of Truth that they know of a surety there is no hope of
salvation for mankind unless He were Himself the Son of the
Virgin who was His mother's Creator. On the other hand this
blasphemous propounder of more recent profanity has confessed the union of the two Natures in Christ, but has maintained that the effect of this very union is that of the two one
remained while the substance of the other no longer existed,
which of course could not have been brought to an end except
by either destruction or separation. But this is so opposed to

sound faith that it cannot be entertained without loss of one's Christian name. For if the Incarnation of the Word is the uniting of the Divine and human natures, but by the very fact of their coming together that which was twofold became single, it was only the Godhead that was born of the Virgin's womb, and went through the deceptive appearance of receiving nourishment and bodily growth: and to pass over all the changes of the human state, it was only the Godhead that was crucified, dead, and buried: so that according to those who thus think, there is no reason to hope for the resurrection, and Christ is not "the first-begotten from the dead"; because He was not One who ought to have been raised again, if He had not been One who could be slain.

VI: Keep far from your hearts, dearly beloved, the poisonous lies of the devil's inspirations, and knowing that the eternal Godhead of the Son underwent no growth while with the Father, be wise and consider that to the same nature to which it was said in Adam, "Thou art earth, and unto earth shall thou go," it is said in Christ, "sit Thou on My right hand." According to that Nature, whereby Christ is equal to the Father, the Only-begotten was never inferior to the sublimity of the Father; nor was the glory which He had with the Father a temporal possession; for He is on the very right hand of the Father, of which it is said in Exodus, "Thy right hand, O Lord, is glorified in power"; and in Isaiah, "Lord, who hath believed our report? and the arm of the Lord, to whom is it revealed?" The man, therefore, assumed into the Son of God, was in such wise received into the unity of Christ's Person from His very commencement in the body, that without the Godhead He was not conceived, without the Godhead He was not brought forth, without the Godhead He was not nursed. It was the same Person in the wondrous acts, and in the endurance of insults; through His human weakness crucified, dead and buried: through His Divine power, being raised the third day, He ascended to the heavens, sat down at the right hand of the Father, and in His nature as man received from the Father that which in His nature as God He Himself also gave.

VII: Meditate, dearly beloved on these things with devout hearts, and be always mindful of the apostle's injunction, who admonishes all men, saying, "See lest any one deceive you through philosophy and vain deceit according to the tradition of men, and not according to Christ; for in Him dwells all the fullness of the Godhead bodily, and ye have been filled in Him." He said not "spiritually" but "bodily," that we may understand the substance of flesh to be real, where there is the dwelling in the body of the fullness of the Godhead: wherewith, of course, the whole Church is also filled, which, clinging to the Head, is the body of Christ; who lives and reigns with the Father and the Holy Ghost, God for ever and ever. Amen.

## DOCUMENTS FROM THE COUNCIL AT CHALCEDON

Since Leo was not in attendance at the Council, a detailed letter was sent to him, both to express appreciation for his teaching, which guided them in their decision, and to inform him of the activities at Chalcedon.

*From the Council of Chalcedon to Leo; date: 451; source: Nicene and Post-Nicene Fathers, Second Series, Vol. XII, 72-73.*

The great and holy and universal Synod, which by the grace of God and the sanction of our most pious and Christ-loving Emperors has been gathered together in the metropolis of Chalcedon in the province of Bithynia, to the most holy and blessed archbishop of Rome, Leo.

I: "Our mouth was filled with joy and our tongue with exultation." This prophecy grace has fitly appropriated to us for whom the security of religion is ensured. For what is a greater incentive to cheerfulness than the Faith? What better inducement to exultation than the Divine knowledge which the Savior Himself gave us from above for salvation, saying, "go ye and make disciples of all the nations, baptizing them into the name of the Father, and of the Son, and of the Holy Ghost, teaching them to observe all things that I have enjoined you"? And this golden chain leading down from the Author of the command to us, you yourself have steadfastly preserved, being set as the mouthpiece unto all of the blessed Peter, and imparting the blessedness of his Faith unto all. Whence we too, wisely taking you as our guide in all that is good,[11] have shown to the sons of the Church their inheritance of Truth, not giving our instruction each singly and in secret, but making known our confession of the Faith in conceit, with one consent and agreement. And we were all delighted, reveling, as at an imperial banquet, in the spiritual food, which Christ supplied to us through your letter: and we seemed to see the Heavenly Bridegroom actually present with us. For if "where two or three are gathered together in His name," He has said that "there He is in the midst of them," must He not have been much more particularly present with 520 priests, who preferred the spread of knowledge concerning Him to their country and their ease? Of whom you were chief, as the head to the members, showing your goodwill in the person of those who represented you; whilst our religious Emperors presided to the furtherance of due order, inviting us to restore the doctrinal fabric of the Church, even as Zerubbabel invited Joshua to rebuild Jerusalem.

II: And the adversary would have been like a wild beast outside the fold, roaring to himself and unable to seize any one, had not the late bishop of Alexandria[12] thrown himself for a prey to him, who, though he had done many terrible things before, eclipsed the former by the latter deeds; for contrary to all the injunctions of the canons, he deposed that blessed shepherd of the saints at Constantinople, Flavian, who displayed such Apostolic faith, and the most pious bishop Eusebius, and acquitted by his terror-won votes

Eutyches, who had been condemned for heresy, and restored to him the dignity which your holiness had taken away from him as unworthy of it, and like the strangest of wild beasts, falling upon the vine which he found in the finest condition, he uprooted it and brought in that which had been cast away as unfruitful, and those who acted like true shepherds he cut off, and set over the flocks those who had shown themselves wolves: and besides all this he stretched forth his fury even against him who had been charged with the custody of the vine by the Savior, we mean of course your holiness, and purposed excommunication against one who had at heart the unifying of the Church. And instead of showing penitence for this, instead of begging mercy with tears, he exulted as if over virtuous actions, rejecting your holiness' letter and resisting all the dogmas of the Truth.[13]

*Chalcedonian Council, Ruling from Session III, Condemnation of Dioscorus; date: 451; source: Nicene and Post-Nicene Fathers, Second Series, Vol. XIV: The Seven Ecumenical Councils (Grand Rapids, MI: Eerdmans, 1957), 260.*

The holy and great and ecumenical Synod, which by the grace of God according to the constitution of our most pious and beloved of God emperors assembled together at Chalcedon the city of Bithynia, in the martyry [a shrine erected to honor a martyr] of the most holy and victorious Martyr Euphemia,[14] to Dioscorus.[15]

We do you to wit that on the thirteenth day of the month of October you were deposed from the episcopate and made a stranger to all ecclesiastical order by the holy and ecumenical synod, on account of your disregard of the divine canons, and of your disobedience to this holy and ecumenical synod[16] and on account of the other crimes of which you have been found guilty, for even when called to answer your accusers three times by this holy and great synod according to the divine canons you did not come.

*Ruling from Session IV; date: 451; Source: Nicene and Post-Nicene
Father, Second Series, Vol. XIV, 260-261.*

Let the reverend council now declare what seems good
concerning the faith, since those things which have already
been disposed of have been made manifest. Paschasinus and
Lucentius, the most reverend bishops, and Boniface the most
reverend presbyter, legates of the Apostolic See through that
most reverend man, bishop Paschasinus[17] said: As the holy and
blessed and Ecumenical Synod holds fast and follows the rule
of faith which was set forth by the fathers at Nicea,[18] it also
confirms the faith set forth by the Synod of 150 fathers gathered
at Constantinople[19] at the bidding of the great Theodosius[20] of
blessed memory. Moreover the exposition of their faith, of the
illustrious Cyril[21] of blessed memory set forth at the Council
of Ephesus[22] (in which Nestorius was condemned) is received.
And in the third place the writings of that blessed man, Leo,
Archbishop of all the churches, who condemned the heresy of
Nestorius and Eutyches, show what the true faith is. Likewise
the holy Synod holds this faith, this it follows—nothing further
can it add nor can it take aught away.

When this had been translated into Greek by Beronician,
the devout secretary of the divine consistory, the most reverend
bishops cried out: So we all believe, so we were baptized, so we
baptize, so we have believed, so we now believe.

The most glorious judges and the great senate said: Since we
see that the Holy Gospels have been placed alongside of your
holiness, let each one of the bishops here assembled declare
whether the epistle of most blessed archbishop Leo is in accordance with the exposition of the 318 fathers assembled at Nicea
and with the decrees of the 150 fathers afterwards assembled
in the royal city.

To this question the bishops answered one by one, until 161
separate opinions had been given, when the rest of the bishops
were asked by the imperial judges to give their votes in a body.[23]
All the most reverend bishops cried out: We all acquiesce, we

all believe thus; we are all of the same mind. So are we minded, so we believe.

*Session V: The Chalcedonian Creed; date: October 22, 451; source: The Creeds of Christendom: Volume II, The Greek and Latin Creeds (Grand Rapids, MI: Baker, 1990), 62-63.*

We, then, following the holy fathers,[24] all with one consent, teach men to confess one and the same Son, our Lord Jesus Christ, the same perfect in Godhead and also perfect in manhood; truly God and truly man, of a reasonable soul and body; consubstantial[25] with the Father according to the Godhead, and consubstantial with us according to the Manhood; in all things like unto us, without sin; begotten before all ages of the Father according to the Godhead, and in these latter days, for us and for our salvation, born of the Virgin Mary, the Mother of God, according to the Manhood; one and the same Christ, Son, Lord, only begotten,[26] to be acknowledged in two natures,[27] inconfusedly, unchangeably, indivisibly, inseparably[28]; the distinction of natures being by no means taken away by the union, but rather the property of each nature being preserved, and concurring in one Person and one Subsistence,[29] not parted or divided into two persons, but one and the same Son, and only begotten, God the Word, the Lord Jesus Christ; as the prophets from the beginning have declared concerning Him,[30] and the Lord Jesus Christ Himself has taught us,[31] and the Creed of the holy Fathers[32] has handed down[33] to us.

# Jesus:
## Yesterday, Today, and Tomorrow

The Nicene and Chalcedonian Creeds provide the church with the orthodox understanding of the person of Christ. These creeds were not the result of ivory-tower theologians debating subtleties. They grew out of the rough and tumble of controversy and even of the persecution that plagued the church. They are the work of the wisdom, patience, and courage of many forgotten figures such as Ignatius, Irenaeus, Athanasius, Basil of Caesarea, Gregory of Nazianzus, Gregory of Nyssa, Flavian of Constantinople, and Leo the Great. These men suffered exile, beatings, the smudging of their character, and even, in the cases of Ignatius and Flavian, death for their full-throttled commitment to the church getting it right on the person of Christ. And they endured it all because they knew that the person of Christ has everything to do with the church's true treasure of the gospel. Christ is the God-man, they all contended, *for us and for our salvation.*

Yet, one may rightly ask how relevant the work of these ancient church fathers from many centuries ago is to life in the church today. To answer this, it might help to look, even briefly, at the intervening centuries between their day and ours. While Chalcedon gave the final and full statement of Christ as the union of the divine and human natures in one person, problems still dogged the church. In the medieval era, debates over Christ's will—did he have a single will or two?—tied theologians in philosophical knots. By the time of the Reformation, however, Arianism once again revealed itself. The uncle and nephew team of Laelius and Faustus Socinius denied the Trinity, denying that Jesus incarnate was the God-man. In their view, Christ became God after the resurrection. They further held that Christ's death on the cross—remember that in their scheme Christ was only human and not God on the cross—does not provide atonement for sins. As God honored Christ's obedience by resurrecting him, God will honor our obedience as we do good works, so they taught.

Arian and Socinian beliefs, though they were not called by that name, made a significant showing in Old and New England in the 1700s and 1800s. In New England, upon the old Puritan soil, Unitarianism quickly engulfed the Congregational churches. When the doctrine of the deity of Christ went, along with it went the doctrine of original sin, the doctrine of the atonement, the doctrine of justification by faith, and the doctrine of hell. They all fell like dominoes.

The doctrine of Christ did not fare well among the deists either. Like the unitarians, the deists held to the absolute oneness of God. Christ was viewed as a prophet, even one who got dangerously close to the divine being. But he wasn't viewed as divine. Benjamin Franklin's famous letter to Ezra Stiles, who happened to be the grandson of Jonathan Edwards, depicts this all too well. Stiles had asked Franklin to put in writing his view of Christ. Franklin acquiesced, confessing:

> As to Jesus of Nazareth, my opinion of whom you particularly desire, I think the system of morals and his religion as he left them to us, the best the world ever saw, or is likely to see, but I apprehend it has received various corrupting changes, and I have with most of the present dissenters in England, some doubts as to his divinity.[1]

At another point, Franklin quipped, "My mother grieves

that one of her sons is an Arminian, another an Arian." Franklin was the latter.

At the turn of the twentieth century in America and Britain especially, liberalism dominated the mainline denominations. In its effort to bring Christianity into the modern world, liberalism waned in its commitment to the Bible, downplaying Christ's miracles, his substitutionary atonement, and his virgin birth. Liberalism wanted to retain these aspects somehow; so it retooled them. But in effect liberalism rejected them all, and in the process rejected the deity of Christ. Liberalism held a high view of Christ, very high. It just couldn't affirm that Christ was the God-man. Speaking precisely to this Achilles' heel of liberalism, J. Gresham Machen put it quite well: "The next thing less than infinite is infinitely less."[2]

Outside of Christianity, broadly and generically understood, Christ has languished even more. The Jehovah's Witnesses famously retranslate John 1:1 to ". . . and the Word was a god" in the futile attempt to argue that Jesus is not equal with God. Many other cults stumble over his deity as well. And then there is Islam. Islam accepts the virgin birth, accepts that Christ performed miracles, accepts that he died on the cross, accepts that he rose from the dead, and even accepts that he is coming again. It rejects, however, the belief that Christ is God. The Koran consistently refers to Christ as "the son of Mary," emphasizing his humanity. The Koran further has Christ constantly submitting to Allah; Christ does everything, he tells Allah, "by your leave."

At one point in the Koran, Surah 5, written about 629, God asks Christ if he ever commanded people to worship him. This is a crucial question to ask. If Christ did command and receive worship, then he is God. Obviously there are such texts in the Gospels. The Koran "cleanses" these corruptions in this section:

> Then God will say, "Jesus, son of Mary, did you ever say to mankind; Worship me and my mother as gods besides God?"

"Glory to you," he will answer, "how could I ever say that to which I have no right? If I had ever said so, You would have surely known it. You know what is in my mind, but I know not what is in yours. You alone know what is hidden. I told them only what you bade me. I said, 'Serve God, my Lord and your Lord.'"

After looking at the intervening centuries between Nicea and Chalcedon and today, it does appear that the ancient creeds have relevance for the church today. These past few years *The Da Vinci Code* troubled the waters. Certainly something else will be following suit. The church should not find itself defenseless in the face of these questions and challenges. Looking to the early church shores up our defense. Even apart from *The Da Vinci Code* phenomenon, people still find Christ a stumbling block. They still get the question Christ put to his disciples—"Whom do you say that I am?"—wrong. They still need the answer that the Nicene and Chalcedonian Creeds declare.

Yet, the value of the Nicene and Chalcedonian Creeds far exceeds that of its apologetic value for those who reject Jesus Christ as God-man, the Word made flesh. These creeds have much value for those in the church. The church is always just one generation away from getting it wrong, from taking a misstep. And getting it wrong on the person of Christ is a fatal misstep. The church of today finds in these fathers of the early centuries the tools, the expressions, the arguments, and the boundaries for the biblical and orthodox view of the person of Christ. We just need to take the time to look.

Paul instructed Timothy to train faithful leaders who would be able to teach others, setting up a line of succession of the passing down and preserving of the gospel (2 Tim. 2:2). This doesn't set up a line of apostolic succession, but it does remind us that we have a tradition of teaching that has been entrusted to us and that we have a responsibility to pass it along to the next generation. The early church labored and sacrificed to ensure that the belief in Christ as fully God and fully human conjoined in one person would prevail. For them this belief was the heart and center of the church's doctrine and practice. We would do well to follow their example, for Christ is the God-man *for us and for our salvation*. And he is the God-man for the salvation of the next generation.

# Glossary

**Adoptionism:** the view that God adopts the human Jesus as his divine son, either at Jesus' birth, baptism, or resurrection.

**Alexandrian:** school of thought associated with theologians at the city of Alexandria, Egypt, from 300 until 450s; spoke of Christ as the word (*Logos*)/flesh (*sarx*); contrasts with Antiochene school.

**Ambrose** (c. 339–397): former imperial governor turned bishop of Milan (374–397); noted preacher and theologian who defended Nicene Christology.

**Anomeans:** from the Greek word *anomoios*, meaning "unlike"; a heretical group that moved beyond Arius, who held that Jesus is similar to the Father, by viewing Jesus as unlike the Father; condemned at the Council of Constantinople in 381.

**Antiochene:** school of thought associated with Antioch, Syria, from 300 until 450s; spoke of Christ as word (*Logos*)/human (*anthropos*); contrasts with Alexandrian school.

**Apelles** (second century): Marcion's disciple in Rome; also traveled to Alexandria; espoused docetism.

**Apollinarius** (c. 315–392): bishop of Laodicea; pro-Nicene theologian who ended up minimizing Christ's humanity; condemned at Council of Chalcedon, 451.

**Arianism:** followers of Arius; though condemned at the Council of Nicea, Arianism maintained a strong presence in the early church until the Council of Constantinople.

**Arius** (c. 260–336): presbyter at Alexandria; denied the deity of Christ, holding Christ to be similar substance (*homoiousion*) with God; condemned at Council of Nicea.

**Athanasius** (c. 300–373): bishop of Alexandria (328–373); defended the deity of Christ by stressing that Christ is of the same substance with (*homoousion*) God; his view finally prevailed at the Council of Constantinople.

**Augustine** (354–430): bishop of Hippo (395–430); towering church father whose writings, numbering over one hundred volumes, are formative for much of Christian theology.

**Basil** (330–379): bishop of Caesarea (370–379); one of the three Cappadocian Fathers; actively refuted Arianism; contributed to development of the doctrine of the Trinity.

**Canon:** the officially recognized books of the Bible; also used to refer to official church documents from councils and synods.

**Cappadocian Fathers:** the three bishops whose cities they served form a triangle in east-central Asia Minor; includes Basil of Caesarea, Gregory of Nazianzus, and Gregory of Nyssa.

**Chalcedon:** city in Asia Minor; host to Council of Chalcedon, held in 451, which affirmed two-nature Christology.

**Chalcedonian Creed:** product of 520 bishops meeting at the Council of Chalcedon in 451; key phrase: Christ is two natures, fully human and fully divine, conjoined in one person; along with the Nicene Creed forms orthodox Christology.

**Christology:** the doctrine of the person and work of Christ.

**Christos:** Greek term meaning "anointed one"; equivalent to Hebrew word meaning "messiah."

**Constantine the Great** (c. 285–337): Roman Emperor (306–337); after his victory at Milvian Bridge (312) he issued a series of edicts legalizing Christianity; called Council at Nicea, 325.

**Constantinople** (Istanbul): capital city, formerly named Byzantium; church councils there include the First Council of Constantinople in 381, the Second Council in 553, and the Third Council in 680.

**Constantius II** (317–361): Roman Emperor (337–361); favored

Arianism and persecuted Athanasius; first to give tax exemption to churches.

**Cyril** (375–444): bishop of Alexandria (412–444); refuted Nestorius; his work contributed to Council of Chalcedon in 451.

**Dioscorus** (?–454): bishop of Alexandria (444–451); enjoying the protection of Theodosius II, upheld the views of Eutyches over those of Flavian; condemned at the Council of Chalcedon.

**Docetism**: from the Greek word *dokeo*, meaning "to appear"; views Christ as only appearing to be human; dominated Christological discussion in the 200s.

**Dyophysitism**: from two Greek words: *dyo* meaning "two" and *physeis* meaning "nature"; the view that Christ has both human and divine natures; affirmed at the Third Council of Constantinople in 680.

**Dyotheletism**: from two Greek words: *dyo* meaning "two" and *thelos* meaning "will"; the view that Christ has both a human and divine will; affirmed at the Third Council of Constantinople in 680.

**Ebionites**: name likely stems from Hebrew word meaning "poor"; a heretical group in the second century who denied the deity of Christ; best seen as attempting to merge Judaism with Christianity.

**Ecumenical Council**: meetings of church leaders that represent the universal (east and west) church; includes seven councils in all from the Council of Nicea in 325 until the Second Council of Nicea in 787.

**Ephesus**: Roman city in Asia Minor; site of Council in 449 that falsely endorsed Eutyches, later overturned at Council of Chalcedon.

**Eunomius** (c. 325–395): bishop of Cyzicus (360–362); became leader of Anomeans, holding Christ to be unlike the Father; condemned at Council of Constantinople in 381.

**Eusebius** (c. 260–c. 339): bishop of Caesarea; as first major historian of the church, he chronicled the early church and the life of Constantine.

**Eutyches** (c. 370–c. 450s): archimandrate (head) of monastery at Constantinople; denied the full humanity of Christ; condemned at Council of Chalcedon.

**Flavian** (?–449): bishop of Constantinople (446–449); died from a beating at the so-called "Robber Council" in Ephesus in 449 for refuting Eutyches; vindicated at Council of Chalcedon.

**Gnosticism**: from Greek word *gnosis*, meaning "knowledge"; borrowing from Platonism, viewed the physical and material as inferior to the immaterial; held to a secret knowledge that would unlock meaning; denied the humanity of Jesus.

**Gregory of Nazianzus** (c. 329–390): bishop of Constantinople (379–381); one of the three Cappadocian Fathers; wrote extensively against Arianism and played a key role at the Council of Constantinople in 381.

**Gregory of Nyssa** (331/340–c. 395): bishop of Nyssa (372–395); brother of Basil of Caesarea and one of the three Cappadocian Fathers; wrote extensively against Arius and Eunomius; was instrumental at the Council of Constantinople in 381.

**Hippolytus** (c. 170–c. 236): theologian and bishop of Rome; wrote significant refutation of docetism and other heresies; writings not attributed to him until discovery in 1551.

*Homoiousion*: compound Greek word from *homoi*, meaning "similar," and *ousion*, meaning "substance" or "essence"; view of Arius, finally condemned at Council of Constantinople in 381.

*Homoousion*: compound Greek word from *homo*, meaning "same" or "identical," and *ousion*, meaning "substance" or "essence"; view of Athanasius, affirmed at Council of Nicea in 325 and again at Council of Constantinople in 381.

**Hypostatic union**: from the Greek word *hypostasis*, meaning "subsistence"; theological term to express that Christ is two natures, human and divine, conjoined in one person; appears in Chalcedonian Creed.

**Ignatius** (b. ?–d. 110s): bishop of Antioch; disciple of John and early martyr; *Epistles* refute early gnostic and docetic heresies, affirming the humanity and deity of Christ.

**Irenaeus** (c. 115–202): bishop of Lyons; writings offer substantial refutations of gnostic heresies; defends authority of four canonical Gospels.

**Judaizers**: generic term that refers to those who conform Christianity to Judaism; denies Christ's deity.

**Leo** (b. ?–d. 461): bishop of Rome (440–461); author of the "Tome," which contains the crucial phrase that Christ is two natures in one person; while not present at the Council of Chalcedon, his "Tome" provided the framework and terminology for the Chalcedonian Creed.

*Logos*: Greek word meaning "word"; the church fathers, playing off the term in John's prologue, used the term as shorthand for the divine nature of Christ.

**Marcellians**: followers of Marcellus of Ancyra (280–374), whose overzealous fight against Arianism led him to view God and Christ (the Word) as entirely identical; condemned at Council of Constantinople in 381.

**Marcian** (392–457): Roman emperor (450–457); called Council of Chalcedon in 451.

**Marcion** (b. ?–d. 154): teacher in Rome; considered leading heretic of second century; interpreted Christianity through Platonism; denied humanity of Christ (among other things).

**Modalism**: heretical view that denies the individual persons of the Trinity; views biblical terminology of God the Father, the Son, and the Holy Spirit as merely modes of existence or manifestations of the one God.

**Monarchianism:** from two Greek words: *mono* meaning "one" and *arche* meaning "ruler"; heretical view that denies the individual persons of the Trinity, instead holding that God is only one.

**Monophysitism:** from two Greek words: *mono* meaning "one" and *physeis* meaning "nature"; expression used by theologians post-Chalcedon who were trying to get around the language of the Chalcedonian Creed; heretical view that Christ possessed a single nature, not distinct human and divine natures.

**Monotheletism:** from two Greek words: *mono* meaning "one" and *thelos* meaning "will"; expression used by theologians post-Chalcedon who were trying to get around the language of the Chalcedonian Creed; heretical view that Christ, while the God-man, possessed a singular will.

**Neoplatonism:** term used to refer to Platonism after the third century, when thinkers mixed concepts and terms from Christianity and Judaism with those of Plato; founder considered to be Plotinus (204–270).

**Nestorius** (c. 381–451): bishop of Constantinople (428–431); his expression of Christ's humanity and deity sounded to many, especially Cyril of Alexandria, as if he was denying that Jesus was one person in favor of seeing Jesus as two persons; condemned at Council of Chalcedon.

**Nicea:** modern-day city of Iznik, Turkey; site of first ecumenical council in 325, called by Constantine to refute the teaching of Arius; also site of seventh ecumenical council in 787.

**Nicene Creed:** product of approximately 300 bishops meeting at the Council of Nicea in 325; key phrase: Christ is of one substance with (*homoousion*) God; along with the Chalcedonian Creed forms orthodox Christology.

**Patripassionism:** from two Greek words: *pater* meaning "father" and *pathos* meaning "suffering"; this view, rejecting the Trinity, holds that it was God the Father who was suffering on the cross in the form of the Son.

**Paul of Samasota** (third century): bishop of Antioch (260–268); denied the preexistence of Jesus, thus denying his deity; condemned at synod of Antioch in 268.

**Plato** (c. 429–347 B.C.): dominant Greek philosopher; his reach extended deeply into the early centuries and the church's formation of theology; held to a low view of matter and the physical world, which gave rise to docetism and gnosticism; his key works influencing the early church include *The Republic* and *Timaeus*.

**Platonism:** the ideas and system of thought of Plato; salient features include the primacy of the ideal forms, a distaste for matter and the physical, and a belief in the creation of the world by the *Demiurge* (meaning Artificer or Creator), who was in turn made by the Ideal (Plato's abstract notion of God).

**Photinians:** followers of Photinus, bishop of Sirmium (c. 344–351); rejected the preexistence of Christ; condemned at the Council of Constantinople in 381.

**Pneumatomochi/Pneumatomachians:** mid-300s heretical group that denied the deity of the Holy Spirit; a splinter group further denied the deity of Christ.

**Sabellianism:** named for Sabellius (third century); heretical view that held Christ to be a mode or manifestation of the Father and not a distinct person; proponents include Noetus and Praxeas.

*Sarx*: Greek word meaning "flesh."

**Socrates Scholasticus** (c. 380–450): church historian who picks up the story where Eusebius leaves off, from 306 until 439.

**Synod:** a meeting of church leaders from a particular region.

**Tertullian** (c. 160–220): leader of church in North Africa; writings provide extensive refutation of early heresies, especially docetism and gnosticism; coined the term *Trinity*, meaning God is three persons, one substance.

**Theodosius I** (346–395): Roman Emperor (379–395); affirmed the views of Athanasius against Arianism; called the Council of Constantinople in 381.

**Theodotus** (second century): gnostic who promoted the views of Valentinus in the eastern church.

**Theodotus the Cobbler** (second century): taught adoptionism at Rome; refuted by Hippolytus.

**Valentinus** (prominent from 120–160): gnostic heretic who taught at Rome; his views may be found in the gnostic text *The Gospel of Truth*, which some scholars think he in fact wrote; held that creation stemmed from the *Pleroma* (Greek word meaning "fullness"), emitting a series of dualities of aeons, one pair of which is the *Logos* and *Sophia*.

# The Doctrine of Christ in Scripture

## KEY TEXTS FOR THE HUMANITY OF CHRIST

*Matthew 1*
*Matthew 4:2-11*
*Luke 2:52*
*Luke 23:26-46*
*John 4:6*

*John 19:28*
*Romans 5:12-21*
*Hebrews 2:10-18*
*Hebrews 4:14-16*

## KEY TEXTS FOR THE DEITY OF CHRIST

*Matthew 28:18-20*
*John 5:18*
*John 8:57-59*
*John 10:22-33*
*Romans 10:8-13*

*1 Corinthians 8:4-6*
*Colossians 1:15-20*
*Hebrews 1:1-4*
*Revelation 5:13-14*

## KEY TEXTS FOR TWO-NATURE CHRISTOLOGY

*Luke 2:11-12*
*John 1:1-18*
*John 20:24-29*
*Acts 2:29-36*

*Romans 1:1-6*
*Philippians 2:5-11*
*Colossians 2:8-10*
*1 Timothy 2:3-6*

# A Guide for Reading the Church Fathers

## BACKGROUND AND REFERENCE WORKS

Chadwick, Henry. *The Early Church* (New York: Penguin, 1993).

Ferguson, Everett. *Backgrounds of Early Christianity*, third edition (Grand Rapids, MI: Eerdmans, 2003).

Hall, Christopher A. *Learning Theology with the Church Fathers* (Downers Grove, IL: InterVarsity Press, 2002).

Kelly, J. N. D. *Early Christian Doctrines*, fifth edition (New York: Continuum, 2000).

Williams, D. H. *Evangelicals and Tradition: The Formative Influence of the Early Church* (Grand Rapids, MI: Baker, 2005).

## PRIMARY SOURCES

*One-volume Works and Readers*

*Early Christian Fathers*, Cyril C. Richardson, Massey Hamilton Shepherd, and Edward Rochie Hardy, eds. (New York: Simon & Schuster, 1995).

*Early Christian Writings*, Maxwell Staniforth, trans. and ed. (New York: Penguin, 1987).

*Eusebius' Ecclesiastical History: Complete and Unabridged*, C. F. Cruse, trans. (Peabody, MA: Hendrickson, 1998).

*Later Christian Fathers: A Selection from the Writings of St. Cyril of Jerusalem to St. Leo the Great*, Henry Bettenson, trans. and ed. (New York: Oxford University Press, 1970).

*Multi-volume Works*

*The Early Church Fathers*, Alexander Roberts, James Donaldson, Philip Schaff, Henry Wace, eds. (Peabody, MA: Hendrickson, 1994 [reprint]). This set was previously published by Eerdmans (1957) and is also available online (www.ccel.org). This set includes the following:

*Ante-Nicene Fathers (ANF), ten volumes:*

Volume 1: Apostolic Fathers, Justin Martyr, Irenaeus

Volume 2: Hermas, Tatian, Athenagoras, Theophilus, Clement of Alexandria

Volume 3: Tertullian

Volume 4: Tertullian (IV), Minucius Felix, Commodian, Origen

Volume 5: Hippolytus, Cyprian, Caius, Novatian, Appendix

Volume 6: Gregory Thaumaturgus, Dionysius the Great, Julius Africanus, Anatolius and Minor Writers, Methodius, Arnobius

Volume 7: Lactantius, Venantius, Asterius, Victorinus, Dionysius, Apostolic Teaching and Constitutions, Homily, and Liturgies

Volume 8: Twelve Patriarchs, Excerpts and Epistles, The Clementina, Apocryphal Gospels and Acts, Syriac Documents

Volume 9: Gospel of Peter, Diatessaron, Testament of Abraham, Epistles of Clement, Origen and Miscellaneous Works

Volume 10: Bibliography, General Index, Annotated Index of Authors and Works

APPENDIX TWO || 161

*Nicene and Post-Nicene Fathers (NPNF), First Series, fourteen volumes*

Volume 1: Augustine: Prolegomena, Confessions, Letters

Volume 2: Augustine: *City of God, Christian Doctrine*

Volume 4: Augustine: Anti-Manichaean, Anti-Donatist Writings

Volume 5: Augustine: Anti-Pelagian Writings

Volume 6: Augustine: Sermon on the Mount, Harmony of the Gospels, Homilies on the Gospels

Volume 7: Augustine: Gospel of John, First Epistle of John, Soliliques

Volume 8: Augustine: Expositions on the Psalms

Volume 9: Chrysostom: On the Priesthood, Ascetic Treatises, Select Homilies and Letters, Homilies on the Statues

Volume 10: Chrysostom: Homilies on the Gospel of St. Matthew

Volume 11: Chrysostom: Homilies on the Acts of the Apostles and the Epistle to the Romans

Volume 12: Chrysostom: Homilies on Corinthians, 1st and 2nd

Volume 13: Chrysostom: Homilies on Galatians, Ephesians, Philippians, Colossians, Thessalonians, Timothy, Titus, and Philemon

Volume 14: Chrysostom: Homilies on the Gospel of John, Hebrews

*Nicene and Post-Nicene Fathers (NPNF), Second Series, fourteen volumes*

Volume 1: Eusebius: Church History, Life of Constantine the Great, Oration in Praise of Constantine

Volume 2: Socrates, Sozomenus: Church Histories

Volume 3: Theodoret, Jerome, Gennadius, Rufinus: Historical Writings

Volume 4: Athanasius: Select Works and Letters

Volume 5: Gregory of Nyssa: Dogmatic Treatises, etc.

Volume 6: Jerome: Letters and Select Works

Volume 7: Cyril of Jerusalem, Gregory Nazianzen
Volume 8: Basil: Letters and Select Works
Volume 9: Hilary of Poitiers, John of Damascus
Volume 10: Ambrose: Select Works and Letters
Volume 11: Sulpitius Severus, Vincent of Lerins, John Cassian
Volume 12: Leo the Great, Gregory the Great
Volume 13: Gregory the Great, Ephraim Syrus, Aphrahat
Volume 14: The Seven Ecumenical Councils

*The Fathers of the Church: A New Translation (Patristic Series)*, Thomas P. Halten, general editor (Washington D. C.: Catholic University of America Press, in process). Currently there are 113 volumes in print or in process. It is an open-ended series, with more volumes projected. This is the new standard scholarly edition in English.

## SELECT BOOKS ON CHRISTOLOGY

Bruce Demarest, *The Cross and Salvation: The Doctrine of Salvation* (Wheaton, IL: Crossway Books, 2006).

Millard Erickson, *The Word Became Flesh: A Contemporary Incarnational Christology* (Grand Rapids, MI: Baker, 1996).

Donald MacLeod, *The Person of Christ* (Downers Grove, IL: InterVarsity Press, 1998).

# Notes

## CHAPTER 1:
## IN THE BEGINNING WAS THE WORD

1. The Koran puts a twist on this by referring to him primarily as "Jesus, Son of Mary," a purposeful underscoring of Islam's rejection of the deity of Christ.

2. See Arnold J. Hultgren and Steven A. Haagmark, eds., *The Earliest Christian Heretics: Readings from Their Opponents* (Minneapolis: Fortress Press, 1996), 116-126.

3. Eusebius, *Church History*, Book VI, Chapter 17, *The Nicene and Post-Nicene Fathers, Second Series, Vol. 1: Eusebius* (Grand Rapids, MI: Eerdmans, 1957), 264.

4. Eusebius, *Church History*, Book V, Chapter 28, 246-248, and Book VII, Chapter 27, 312.

5. The terms *monarchianism, modalism, patripassionism,* and *Sabellianism* are used interchangeably in referring to this heresy. See Tertullian's work *Against Praxeas.*

6. Tertullian, "On the Flesh of Christ," Chapter 1, *Ante-Nicene Fathers, Vol. 3: Tertullian* (Grand Rapids, MI: Eerdmans, 1957), 521. For Plato's idealism, see his *Republic.*

7. Incidentally, some credit Christianity as instituting male chauvinism. As can be seen from this rundown of Plato, he's the guilty party. Furthermore, when set against the backdrop of the Platonist's view of women as inferior beings, the Bible stands out for its anti-male-chauvinist stance. Adam may have been created before Eve, but both are in the image of God. Paul's teaching of ontological unity and equality of the genders starkly contrasts with Plato's understanding of the genders.

8. Again, see Plato's *Republic* for his theory of the forms.

9. Irenaeus, *Against the Heresies*, Book I.

10. Ibid., Book I, Chapter 7.

11. Tertullian, *Against Marcion*, Book III, Chapter 8.

12. As Ignatius traveled to Rome, he composed seven letters. Polycarp,

bishop of Smyrna, compiled these letters, and they were widely circulated in the early church. Scholars doubt the authenticity of other letters beyond these seven that have been attributed to him. See Ivor J. Davidson, *The Birth of the Church: From Jesus to Constantine, AD 30–312* (Grand Rapids, MI: Baker, 2004), 181-182.

13. Ignatius, "The Epistle of Ignatius to the Trallians," *The Ante-Nicene Fathers, Volume I: The Apostolic Fathers with Justin Martyr and Irenaeus*, A. Cleveland Coxe, ed. (Grand Rapids, MI: Eerdmans, 1957), 66-72.

14. See Dennis Means, "Truth and Tradition: Irenaeus," *Cambridge History of Christianity: Origins to Constantine*, Margaret M. Mitchell and Frances M. Young, eds. (Cambridge: Cambridge University Press, 2006), 261-273.

15. Irenaeus, *Against Heresies*, Book I, Chapter X, *The Ante-Nicene Fathers, Volume I*, 330. For a discussion of the text of *Against Heresies*, see Richard A. Norris, Jr., "Irenaeus of Lyon," *The Cambridge History of Early Christian Literature*, Frances Young, Lewis Ayres, and Andrew Loith, eds. (Cambridge: Cambridge University Press, 2004), 45-52.

16. See A. Cleveland Coxe, "Introductory Notice to Hippolytus," *The Ante-Nicene Fathers, Vol. V: Hippolytus* (Grand Rapids, MI: Eerdmans, 1957), 7.

17. Hippolytus, *Refutation of All Heresies*, Book X, Chapters 29-30, *The Ante-Nicene Fathers, Vol. V: Hippolytus*, 150-153. For a scholarly discussion of Hippolytus and his writings, see "Hippolytus, Ps.-Hippolytus and the Early Canons," *The Cambridge History of Early Christian Literature*, 142-151.

## CHAPTER 2:
## IN THEIR OWN WORDS: SELECT DOCUMENTS FROM THE EARLY CENTURIES

1. In keeping with Plato's understanding of the world, the author(s) of *The Gospel of Thomas* consider the physical world a "corpse"; true reality lies beyond it.

2. This is a curious Trinitarianism: the mouth of the Father is Christ, the "embodiment" of truth, and the tongue is the Holy Spirit.

3. The crucial word here is *form*; Jesus was not truly in the flesh.

4. Ignatius is using his own willingness to suffer as a disciple of Christ

as an argument for Christ's real suffering in his humanity. It would be vain for Ignatius to physically suffer if Christ did not suffer.

5. Ignatius connects his view of the person of Christ to the work of Christ.

6. Ignatius walks his readers through the very confusing maze of the "aeons" as understood by the Valentinians. Borrowing from Plato's theory of the forms, they constructed an elaborate scheme of beings that all descend in pairs from the "Pleroma" or fullness. The Valentinians refer to these various beings, such as Sophia, referred to here as "Achamoth," and the Demiurge (creator), with biblical terminology.

7. Irenaeus counters the Valentinian understanding with the proper biblical teaching of Christ.

8. An "Ogdoad" is a group of eight divine beings or aeons in Valentinian gnosticism.

9. Irenaeus directly connects Christ, as the Word made flesh, to Adam. This view of Christ's humanity is important for Christ's work. Christ will undo, through his perfect obedience, what Adam did, through his disobedience, in the arena of humanity. The Gnostic Christ is a being outside of humanity, which has significant implications for Christ's work on the cross.

10. These terms are transliterations of Greek words: *Logos* = "word"; *Monogenes* = "only begotten"; *Zoe* = "life"; *Phos* = "light"; *Soter* = "Savior"; *Christus* = "Christ" (Messiah).

11. Irenaeus was quite aware of the various gnostic gospels circulating in the early church. He flatly rejects them in favor of the four Gospels, which he famously refers to as the "four pillars." This evidence creates significant problems for the arguments of some current scholars, such as Bart Ehrman in his *Lost Christianities: The Battle for Scripture and the Faith We Never Knew* (New York: Oxford University Press, 2005) and *Lost Scripture: Books that Did Not Make It into the Bible* (New York: Oxford University Press, 2005) and Elaine Pagels in her *Beyond Belief: The Secret Gospel of Thomas* (New York: Vintage Books, 2003). Ehrman and Pagels, with many others, contend that all of these texts—both the canonical and gnostic gospels—shared equal footing in the early centuries.

12. Tertullian's statement reveals docetism as the dominant heresy plaguing the church in the second and third centuries.

13. Tertullian proceeds to name three docetists in particular—Marcion, Apelles, and Valentinus.

14. Tertullian states Marcion's heresy succinctly: Marcion did not view Christ as human, as flesh and blood, but as a phantom.

15. Tertullian makes the connection between the person of Christ and the work of Christ. Marcion's Christ is not a sufficient sacrifice for sinful humanity.

16. Hippolytus contends that Valentinus's system is borrowed from Pythagoras and Plato. Like a clever plagiarizer, Valentinus merely changed a few terms, exchanging Plato's names, like "Monad," for biblical ones, like "God" and "Father."

17. Here at the end of Book X Hippolytus turns from explaining and refuting heresies to positively setting forth the Christian belief in Christ.

## CHAPTER 3:
## THE TRIUMPH OF ATHANASIUS: THE BATTLE FOR CHRIST AT NICEA

1. Dan Brown, *The Da Vinci Code* (New York: Random House, 2003), Chapter 55.

2. For a discussion of the different numbers of bishops in attendance at Nicea, see R. P. C. Hanson, *The Search for the Christian Doctrine of God: The Arian Controversy, 318–381*(Grand Rapids, MI: Baker Academic, 2005), 155-156. After weighing the evidence, Hanson concludes, "All that we can say is that the number of bishops at the Council of Nicea probably fell between 250 and 300," 156.

3. For the canons of the Council of Nicea, see *The Nicene and Post-Nicene Fathers, Second Series, Volume XIV: The Seven Ecumenical Councils of the Undivided Church*, Henry R. Percival, ed. (Grand Rapids, MI: Eerdmans, 1956), 1-56. This book also contains the canons and creeds of the other six ecumenical councils as well as from the many synods that occurred from 300 until 787 and the seventh council, also held at Nicea. The Roman Catholic Church continues to convene councils, the last being Vatican II, 1962–1965. Since the split of the Roman Catholic Church (the so-called "Western Church") from Greek Orthodoxy (the so-called "Eastern Church") in 1054, these councils are not considered "ecumenical," since each side refuses to recognize the other.

4. J. Gresham Machen, *What Is Faith?* (Carlisle, PA: The Banner of Truth Trust, 1991), 116.

5. For more on Athanasius's struggles for orthodoxy and what the church of today can learn from it, see John Piper, *Contending for Our All: Defending Truth and Treasuring Christ in the Lives of Athanasius, John Owen, and J. Gresham Machen* (Wheaton, IL: Crossway Books, 2006), 38-75.

6. Anthony Meredith, S.J., *Gregory of Nyssa* (London: Routledge, 1999), 2.

7. Gregory, "Correspondence with Saint Basil the Great," Epistle I, *The Nicene and Post-Nicene Fathers, Second Series, Vol. VII: S. Cyril of Jerusalem and S. Gregory of Nazianzen* (Grand Rapids, MI: Eerdmans, 1957), 446.

8. One poem by Gregory of Nazianzus offers an autobiographical sketch. See also the introduction to his life and work by Charles Gordon Browne and James Edward Swallow in *Nicene and Post-Nicene Fathers, Second Series, Vol. VII*, 187-200.

9. Gregory, "Correspondence with Saint Basil the Great," Epistle VIII and Epistle XIX, *Nicene and Post-Nicene Fathers, Second Series, Vol. VII*, 448.

10. Ambrose, "On the Death of Theodosius," reprinted in *Christianity in Late Antiquity 300–450 C.E.: A Reader*, Bart D. Ehrman and Andrew S. Jacobs, eds. (Oxford: Oxford University Press, 2004), 57.

11. Eusebius, *The Life of Constantine*, Book I, Chapter 24, *Nicene and Post-Nicene Fathers, Second Series, Vol. 1: Eusebius* (Grand Rapids, MI: Eerdmans, 1957), 489.

## CHAPTER 4:
## IN THEIR OWN WORDS: SELECT DOCUMENTS FROM THE FOURTH CENTURY

1. Prior to Constantine, the church experienced one of the most trying waves of persecution at the hands of Diocletian.

2. Licinius was emperor in the east from 308–324. At the end of his reign, Constantine ruled a united empire from 324–337.

3. Beginning with the Edict of Milan, 313, Constantine issued a series of edicts that first legalized, then privileged Christianity.

4. Athanasius draws attention to the need of the incarnation. Humanity, having sinned against God, is in a corrupt state. It

would be incongruous with God's character, mainly his goodness, to leave humanity in a corrupt state without a means of redemption.

5. This refers to Arius's view that Christ was created by God and is therefore less than God.

6. Eusebius, bishop of Caesarea and early church historian, while not siding with Arius, was concerned to acknowledge a degree of superiority for the Father. Athanasius refers to him as heterodox, not as a heretic, which he reserved for Arius. Eusebius's concerns for seeing a hierarchy in the Trinity led him to overstate the matter, which raised Athanasius's concerns.

7. Athanasius uses Paul's link of Christ with God the Father in creating the world (1 Corinthians 8:6) as an argument against Arius's view that Christ was created.

8. The declaration that Jesus is the same essence (*homoousion*) as the Father is the decisive statement in the Nicene Creed.

9. This text paints the picture of the persecution of the orthodox bishops at the hands of the Arian bishops and the magistrates.

10. Athanasius fled so as to avoid certain persecution.

11. Athanasius was able to disguise himself and elude his would-be captors.

12. Emperor Julian, who ruled a united empire from 361–363, had ordered the governor of Alexandria to capture Athanasius.

13. In this first chapter Basil admits the controversy concerns minutiae and complex subtleties, which he refers to as "syllables." Nevertheless, he contends that this minutiae, which concerns how the church speaks of the Trinity, is of utmost importance.

14. Basil poetically describes the turmoil in the church caused by these Chistological and Trinitarian controversies.

15. Gregory states that he will not give in to the pressure to espouse Arian beliefs and thus avoid persecution.

16. Gregory declares the three members of the Godhead to be equal in essence; each one is God.

17. The two first became friends as students at the University of Athens.

18. Eunomius was bishop of Cyzicus from 361–364. An extreme Arian, he taught that Christ was unlike the Father since the Father had created him. The Greek word for *unlikeness* is *anomoion*.

This term became the name of the followers of this teaching, the Anomoeans.

19. Gregory follows many in this time who held Paul to be the author of Hebrews; the anonymity of Hebrews caused problems for its acceptance as canonical.

20. Gregory affirms that Christ is fully and absolutely equal with the Father.

21. Arius takes the reference to Christ as "begotten" to mean that Christ was created. Since Christ was created, he was not eternal and therefore not exactly or identically like the Father. In this letter Arius, claiming to be unjustly pursued, downplays the problem of his view and his guilt.

22. This is the crucial statement of Nicea. Arius's view holds that Christ is of similar substance (*homoiousion*) with the Father. The Nicene Council sided with Athanasius, affirming that Christ is of identical substance with the Father.

23. While the Arian view was condemned at Nicea, the political tide would change in 337 after the death of Constantine and the rise to power of Constantius II. Ironically, from the 330s until 381 and the Council of Constantinople, it would be the so-called Nicene bishops who would suffer and the Arian bishops who would have the upper hand.

24. Later western editions of this creed added the phrase, "and the Son" (*filioque* in Latin) in relation to the Spirit's procession. It appears as early as 400 and took on synodal status in Spain by 589. In 1014 it was first officially used in Rome. In 1054 this little phrase, merely one word in Latin, split the church into east (the Orthodox Church), which rejected it outright, and west (the Roman Catholic Church), which by now had incorporated the phrase into the Creed.

## CHAPTER 5:
## THE WISDOM OF LEO THE GREAT: THE BATTLE FOR CHRIST AT CHALCEDON

1. For a moving version of Bach's *Mass in B Minor*, try Deutsche Grammaphone's recording of the Berliner Philharmoniker, conducted by Herbert Von Karajan, 1974.

2. See also Donald Macleod, *The Person of Christ* (Downers Grove, IL: InterVarsity Press, 1998), 181-203; Ivor J. Davidson, *A Public Faith: From Constantine to the Medieval World, AD 312-600*

(Grand Rapids, MI: Baker, 2005), 195-215; and Everett Ferguson, *Church History: Volume One, From Christ to Pre-Reformation* (Grand Rapids, MI: Zondervan, 2005), 255-267.

3. E. A. Thompson, *The Huns* (London: Blackwell, 1996), 161.

4. See Paul Parvis, "Nestorianism," *Jesus in History, Thought, & Culture: An Encyclopedia, Vol. Two, K-Z*, Leslie Houlden, ed. (Santa Barbara, CA: ABC-CLIO, 2003), 637-643.

5. For more on the debate between the Antiochene and Alexandrian schools, see Alister E. McGrath, *Historical Theology: An Introduction to the History of Christian Thought* (Oxford: Blackwell Publishers, 1998), 51-61.

6. Leo, Sermon XXIII, "On the Feast of the Nativity, III," *Nicene and Post-Nicene Fathers, Second Series, Vol. XII: Leo the Great* (Grand Rapids, MI: Eerdmans, 1957), 133; Dietrich Bonhoeffer, *Christ the Center* (New York: Harper Collins, 1978), 104.

7. Leo's "Tome," or Letter XXVIII to Flavian, *Nicene and Post-Nicene Fathers, Second Series, Vol. XII*, 40, 45.

8. Leo, Sermon XLVI, "On Lent, VIII," ibid., 59.

9. See Leo's sermon series on the Feasts of the Nativity, Sermons XXI–XXVII, especially Sermon XXIII, ibid., 132-134.

10. Leo, Sermon XXI, ibid., 128.

11. Ibid., 129.

## CHAPTER 6:
## IN THEIR OWN WORDS: SELECT DOCUMENTS FROM THE FIFTH CENTURY

1. Eutyches, enjoying the favor of the emperor, would be victorious over Flavian at the so-called "Robber Council," only to be condemned at Chalcedon in 451. While Flavian proceeds to reference the heresies of Nestorianism and Apollinarianism, Eutychianism dominated this correspondence between Flavian and Leo.

2. The Nicene Creed.

3. Cyril (375–444), bishop of Alexandria, was instrumental at the Council of Ephesus in 431, which condemned Nestorius.

4. Eutyches, in his attempt to express how the divine and human natures come together in the person of Christ, ended up compromising the full humanity of Christ. This view put him at odds with

the Nicene Creed, referred to by Flavian as "the expositions of the holy fathers."

5. This is the crucial section of the "Tome," in which Leo expresses the two-nature Christology. He further underscores how Christ as the God-man, in the incarnation, has everything to do with his work on the cross, the atonement.

6. Leo insists on the two-nature doctrine, stressing that it bears repeating and emphasizing.

7. Here Leo counsels Flavian on how to answer Eutyches directly. Eutyches was arguing that at the incarnation, Jesus no longer had two distinct and intact natures.

8. These emissaries represented Leo at the "Robber Council," where they were physically beaten, and also at the Council of Chalcedon.

9. This letter is a shorter statement of Leo's ideas in the "Tome." It was written to a group of monks to guard them against the false teachings of the Eutychians, whom he refers to colorfully as "phantom-mongers."

10. Philippians 2, cited here, took on more and more significance in the Christological controversy. This text served as the touchstone for Leo and Chalcedon's two-nature Christology.

11. This refers to Leo's "Tome," which was read at the Council and served as the basis for the Chalcedonian Creed.

12. Dioscorus was the bishop who exonerated Eutyches at the "Robber Council" and had Flavian, and anyone who supported him, beaten into submission, which this letter refers to as "terror-won votes." Flavian died from the beating.

13. Dioscorus refused to allow Leo's emissaries to read his "Tome" at the council in Ephesus in 449. When Leo heard of the abuses at this council, he termed it a "Robber Council" (*Latrocinium*).

14. Euphemia was an early martyr in the city of Chalcedon and was taken as a sort of patron saint of the city.

15. Dioscurus, bishop of Alexandria.

16. Dioscorus refused to appear before the council at Chalcedon when summoned.

17. Paschasinus, bishop of Lilybaeum in Sicily. He went to Chalcedon as one of Leo's representatives, acting as chief spokesperson.

18. The Nicene Creed, 325.

19. The Council of Constantinople, 381.

20. Theodosius I, emperor in the east from 379–395.

21. Cyril of Alexandria.

22. 431.

23. With 359 names to go, they stopped the roll call at number 161, settling for a voice vote.

24. "Holy fathers" is a reference to the bishops at Nicea and the Nicene Creed.

25. The Greek word is *homoousion*, Athanasius's key word from the Nicene Creed that means "identical substance or essence."

26. Up to this point the Chalcedonian Creed is essentially reaffirming the Nicene Creed.

27. This is the contribution of Chalcedon to the development of Christology: that Christ is two natures, human and divine, in one person.

28. These four words were carefully chosen to refute the heresies of Apollinarius, Nestorius, and Eutyches.

29. The Greek word translated "Subsistence" is *hypostasis*. Theologians use that word to refer to the *hypostatic union*, the union of the fully divine and fully human natures in the one person, Christ.

30. This phrase refers to the Old Testament.

31. This phrase refers to the Gospels and the New Testament.

32. This phrase refers to the Nicene Creed.

33. The Greek word is *karadedwke*, which means "to entrust" or "to hand down" (see 2 Timothy 2:2). The Latin word is *tradidit*, from which we get the English word *tradition*.

## EPILOGUE:
## JESUS: YESTERDAY, TODAY, AND TOMORROW

1. Benjamin Franklin to Ezra Stiles, March 9, 1790.

2. J. Gresham Machen, *What Is Faith?* (Carlisle, PA: The Banner of Truth, 1991), 116. See also Stephen J. Nichols, *J. Gresham Machen: A Guided Tour of His Life and Thought* (Phillipsburg, NJ: P&R, 2004), 99-116.